Zen

and the

Art of

Systems Analysis

It's Easy to be Great TV Shows!

Book one in the *Zen Analyst* series.

Also by Patrick McDermott:

Workflow Modeling
Tools for Process Improvement and Application Development
(With Alec Sharp)

The Systems Analyst as Internal Consultant

Karate's Supreme Ultimate
The Taikyoku Kata in Five Rings
(With Ferol Arce)

Zen

and the

Art of

Systems Analysis

Meditations on Computer Systems Development

Patrick McDermott

Writers Club Press
New York Lincoln Shanghai

Zen and the Art of Systems Analysis
Meditations on Computer Systems Development

Writers Club Press
an imprint of iUniverse, Inc.

For information address:
iUniverse, Inc.
2021 Pine Lake Road, Suite 100
Lincoln, NE 68512
www.iuniverse.com

Second Revised Printing, 2003

ISBN: 0-595-25679-1 (Pbk)
ISBN: 0-595-65255-7 (Cloth)
ISBN: 0-595-75230-6 (eBook)

Printed in the United States of America

The Meditating Buddha, the quintessence of Zen and an inspiration for the deep thought of the systems analyst, is always shown seated on a Lotus, a beautiful lily that grows from the muck of the swamp bottom. This book is dedicated to another beautiful flower of the Lily Family.

Lilian

Having the greatest respect for the followers of that great body of wisdom known as esoteric Zen Buddhism whose tenets I expound throughout this book, I hope they will take the book in the spirit of reverence in which it was written, especially since this wisdom is often expressed through proficiency in martial arts!

—Patrick McDermott

Contents

Preface

This contract limits our liability—Read it carefully!

After two decades as an avid systems analyst, obsessed computer programmer, and reluctant programming manager, I began my own consulting firm, specializing in training, teaching and writing. When teaching, I try to give battle-tested tips, and tell eclectic stories to illustrate my points (and see if anyone's awake). I decided to collect some of them into this book.

Occasionally, when asked about some play or movie, I've realized that although I had disliked it at first, it passed the think test: I had found myself thinking about it in the days that followed. And so I hope with this book. It does not always have answers, often just more questions. You might love it or you might hate it, but if you find yourself thinking about it later, I've been successful.

These stories don't always give an explicit moral—usually because I don't know what the moral is, yet. I've been free with my opinions, some of which I even agree with, and try to share a certain offbeat thought process. You should think from analogy, and even life generally, so many of these stories might not immediately seem to relate directly to information systems analysis.

And you'll find lots of contradictions here. Like any good list of aphorisms, some are opposites. You'll find impossible proverbs, parable paradoxes, fighting fables, contradictory *kotowaza*, and muddy maxims: Don't bite off more than you can chew—but if you aim for the stars you might reach the moon; Look before you leap—but he who hesitates is lost; You snooze, you lose—but sleep on it.

I didn't do extensive research, so some are apocryphal stories, which I define as stories that *should* be true even if they aren't. I lived in Texas when in grade school, so I appreciate the tall tale, and my Irish heritage would never let the truth ruin a good story.

So the book is nebulous, ambiguous, and filled with off-topic and contradictory stories that might not even be true.

Come to think of it, that pretty much describes a systems analyst's life!

Introduction

My father was in the U.S. Air Force, so my family lived in many places. My first memories in life are of the Philippine Islands, and I went to Kubasaki Junior High and High Schools in Okinawa, Japan. I was fortunate to have lived off the military base in downtown Naha, and so had closer contact with the culture of the East than most of my classmates. After some years as a systems analyst, burnt-out, I moved to Tokyo for six months to re-new myself, and deepened my acquaintance with Japanese culture, history and philosophy. I was struck by the applicability of many of Eastern philosophy's beliefs to computers.

It's surprising how many Japanese concepts are already in English. For example, that incontestable intellectual and social arbiter, the Microsoft Word ® Spellchecker, acccpts as normal English words: aikido, anime, banzai, bushido, daimyo, dojo, geisha, hara-kiri, judo, jujitsu, jujutsu, kaizen, kamikaze, kana, kanji, karaoke, karate, keiretsu, kendo, kimono, kohai, ninja, origami, samurai, sashimi, sempai, sensei, seppuku, shogun, sushi, tsunami, zaibatsu, and of course Zen. I am not Zen Buddhist by religion, but I do agree with many Eastern ideas and tenets, and have found them surprisingly helpful in analysis, and so I use them as a theme throughout this book.

Our Three Guiding Principles

The central tenet of Buddhism is: There is suffering in the World; which has a cause; and can end. The way to end suffering is laid out in the Noble Eight-fold Path. All analysts know there is always suffering involved in the quest for a good system. Thinking this book might reduce the suffering of the long-suffering systems analysts who read it, I chose the Eight-fold path as a more-or-less arbitrary organizational theme for the book. The book is organized into eight chapters around the eight topics in the chapter titles, loosely paralleling the Noble Eight-Fold Path. Thank you for taking this journey with me. Before we start, we'll ponder the Three Guiding Principles that underlie Systems Analysis and this book: The Middle Way; Embrace Contradiction; and the Many Ways to the Mountaintop. These three principles affect much we will talk about throughout this book.

THREE PRINCIPLES

1. Choose the Middle Way.
2. Embrace Contradiction.
3. There are Many Ways to the Mountaintop.

---

1. Choose the Middle Way

The first principle is that of the Middle Way. The principle advises avoiding extremes. Although not reported to be a practicing Buddhist, Goldilocks understood the principle well. Imagine her looking at some Entity-Relationship Diagrams (ERDs): "This ERD is too sketchy"; "This ERD is too detailed"; "This ERD is *ju-u-u-ust right*." Much of this book will involve finding a middle way between two extremes. For example, you must thoroughly analyze every situation while avoiding analysis paralysis. For specifications, tests, and edits—almost everything—you must copy Goldilocks and get it *just right*. By following the middle way, you will avoid extremes, as they are rarely the best way, and by finding the middle ground between two competing ideas, you can get the best of both.

2. Embrace Contradiction

Soto Zen Master Taisen Deshimaru (1914-1982) said, "Harmonizing opposites by going back to their source is the distinctive quality of the Zen attitude, the Middle Way: embracing contradictions, making a synthesis of them, achieving balance." Life is a contradiction, and the cosmos is oxymoronic. *Oxymoron* is constructed from the Greek words meaning sharp and dull. Sounds like a contradiction, both sharp and dull at the same time. So an oxymoron is a phrase that has a seeming contradiction, but in fact often contains a profound truth. Shakespeare was right: Parting *is* such sweet sorrow, although sorrow is certainly not sweet. Be careful with the word, because if you call someone who doesn't know the meaning of the word "oxymoronic" you might get punched, but to a true Zen analyst, oxymoronic is a great compliment.

As a systems analyst you must embrace contradiction. Systems analysis *is* contradiction. In fact, it's a riddle inside a conundrum that's part of a mysterious puzzle. Remember, genius is the ability to hold two completely contradictory opinions at the same time. As with The Force in the *Star Wars* movies, you must learn to trust your intuition, and let your gut guide you when your head can't.

Beware the nagging question. If you feel uneasy, there's probably a reason, and in analysis, minor contradictions can lead to major consequences later. If there is something you don't understand there must be something wrong. So you must dig and dig until you resolve the issue. You're in peril if your gut disagrees with your head.

Wait! Isn't that the opposite of what I just said in the previous paragraph? So what should you do, accept a contradiction and live with it, or not proceed until you eliminate it??? The answer, of course, is "Yes".

3. There are Many Ways to the Mountaintop

After years of research, computer science has finally discovered the one true best methodology—at least a hundred of them, in fact! Each guru will tell you his is the only way, but no way is always right. When asked to compare various methods of attaining enlightenment, the Buddha is said to have remarked: "There are many ways to the Mountaintop." Some are harder, and some are easier; some are surer, some slipperier. But many ways are valid. You must find your own best way, but one of the first things to learn in the analyst business: You've got to be flexible. There is no one correct, or even best, methodology—or technique, or tool, or approach. The rub of course is that although there is no one right way, there are in fact many wrong ways, and the essence of analysis is avoiding them. So this book contains tips and rules of thumb to help you determine which approach to embrace and which to avoid. An idea is a very dangerous thing if you only have one.

Notes

The medical missionary Dr. James C. Hepburn invented the method of transliterating Japanese into Roman characters that I generally use in the book to render Japanese into English, except when usage has developed otherwise. Unfortunately, this method has some ambiguities and difficulties, one of which is the need to show a macron to distinguish the pronunciation of long vowels. Those unfamiliar with spoken Japanese find the macrons (ō, ū) distracting, but they are essential to correct pronunciation. As a compromise, I am generally careful to show the macrons on the first or defining occurrence of a word but less exacting on subsequent occurrences. I do this out of my great concern for the reader, and because it's easier to leave them off and I'm lazy. In this book, the first or defining occurrence of a Japanese word will be italicized and show the macrons; thereafter it will be treated as an English word, without macrons, except following the Japanese, which does not have grammatical plurals, the plural form is the same as the singular.

I considered formal references but since my readers all buy their books on-line, if you need one you can look it up on Amazon.com yourself. There is a Bibliography provided that lists the books mentioned in the text that I think you might find helpful (Hint to Jeff Bezos: to cite a book in a scholarly work, we also need the *city* it was published in. Could that be on the wishlist for the next release?)

1

NIRVANA THROUGH ANALYSIS

Human salvation lies in the hands of the creatively
maladjusted.
—Martin Luther King, Jr.

Step One on the Eight-Fold Path to Technological Enlightenment is to
gain the Right Understanding. Analysts seek understanding, so Chapter
1 covers analysis, creativity, and especially thinking like an analyst. It
talks about tools, but mostly tries to loosen your mind to get you outside that proverbial box everyone has been thinking inside of. It even
shows you where the box is.

Nirvana, or in Japanese *satori*, is the state of sublime understanding. It's
not a place, but a mode of thought—Daisetz Suzuki tells us of satori that
"The object of Zen discipline consists in acquiring a new viewpoint for
looking into the essence of things"—as concise an explanation of thinking
like an analyst as I've ever read. So in this section you'll learn to think like a
Systems Analyst in order to reach the nirvana of systems understanding.
You need to get into a certain mode of thought to be a good analyst, and
sometimes need to look at the world a little differently.

Getting Started

The first step is often the hardest step in solving any problem. When my programming students get stuck on an assignment, I usually tell them "You might not know how to solve the problem, but you do know how to do *something* needed for the solution." In other words, if you don't know how to do it, don't you know how to do *part* of it? You don't know how to do the calculation, but you know you'll have to input data. Start with that. The Japanese have a proverb: *Sen ri no michi mo ippo kara*: "Even a journey of a thousand miles starts from one step", and it's absolutely true when undertaking analysis or moving to on to any new phase in the SDLC (System Development Life Cycle—see Chapter 7).

> **Sen Ri no Michi mo Ippo kara**
> **"Even a Journey of a Thousand Miles**
> **starts from One Step"**

The strategy is to divide and conquer. Break the problem into bite size pieces. Anne Lamott has written a delightful book on writing called *Bird by Bird: Some Instructions on Writing and Life*. The title came from a childhood incident when her young brother needed to write an essay about ornithology, and felt overwhelmed by the work ahead. The advice the author's father gave to him: "Just take it bird by bird." So, if you need to get started, but feel overwhelmed, just take it step by step, interview by interview, module by module, bird by bird.

Yin & Yang

Yin and Yang, called Inyō in Japanese, is denoted by the symbol called Taikyoku in Japanese, T'ai Chi in Chinese. Taikyoku is also the name of a kata in Karate, and a slow-moving Chinese martial art. The symbol's on the cover of this book, and looks like this:

Yin and Yang are represented by the dark and light areas in the circle. Notice there is a little piece of light in the dark, and vice versa. This is because there is always a little bit of Yin in every Yang: there is light within dark, strong within the weak, good in evil, and vice versa. These Yin/Yang pairs are sometimes called opposites, but that is not accurate—they are actually complementary. One could not exist without the other. A young martial artist then living in Oakland, California, explained this in his 1963 book: "The 'one-ness' of Yin/Yang is necessary in life. If a person riding a bike wishes to go somewhere, he cannot pump on both pedals at the same time or not pump on them at all. In order to move forward, he has to pump one pedal and release the other. So the movement of going forward requires this 'oneness' of pumping and releasing." Incidentally, this particular martial artist later left Oakland to pursue a career in entertainment, of all things. I heard he even made a couple of movies. His name was Bruce Lee.

Sensei Ferol Arce of Wado Ki Kai Karate Dojo tells us a punch is made more effective by the retreating hand, so both the so-called yin and yang hands are critical to the technique. In fact, the retreating hand should be thought of as an attack—an elbow strike to the rear. Likewise, your system will need to blend business with technology, people with machines, and analysis with design if it is to succeed. Some systems analysts argue: "Analysis does not include design. You must never let design enter your mind during analysis." I've always found this profoundly silly. Imagine someone telling you he has just completed a thorough analysis of a vehicle:

"What kind of vehicle?" you ask him.

"I don't know, that's a design issue and I *analyzed* the vehicle", he replies.

So you ask: "Well, what will it be used for?"

"I have no idea, that's a design question and I was doing analysis", he replies.

You probe further: "Does it roll, or fly, or float?"

"Beats me, that's about design and I did an analysis", he replies.

Etc., etc., etc.

This obviously makes no sense: you can't analyze something if you don't even know what it's used for. Likewise with your analysis, there will always be some analysis in your design, and design in your analysis (Yin and Yang).

The Unpleasant and the Difficult

Tasks that are hard to accomplish can be grouped into two categories: unpleasant work, and difficult work. Embrace contradiction: Opposite approaches are needed for these two categories. For the unpleasant, the Nike motto is best: "Just do it". It's not going to get any better, so get it over with; the time you'll spend dreading it will increase the total unpleasantness, so unless you can avoid it permanently (probably the best approach of all), get it over with.

For the difficult, the approach is reversed. Use the Power of Positive Procrastination. Sleep on it. Let it sit in your subconscious for a while. Do some thinking about it from time to time, but delay the decision as long as possible. If no answer is required for several weeks, start a folder on the problem, then put it aside. Pick up the folder every few days and think about it a little, but don't force it. A certain Zen acolyte was given an especially tricky *koan*, a difficult riddle as an exercise to help him gain understanding. When he asked how long it would take to master the koan, he was told, "About two years". "But what if I study really, really hard?" "Then it will take you about twenty years!" was the reply.

> **Over time,**
> **Unpleasant tasks become *more* unpleasant, but**
> **Difficult tasks become *less* difficult.**

One technique for managing difficult questions in meetings and facilitated sessions is the parking lot. It allows you to defer difficult questions in the hope they will resolve themselves. In this technique, you take a sheet of paper or board and label it "Parking Lot". When something comes up you can't resolve, simply note it on a Post-It note and place it on the parking lot. Since it's visible, and will be taken care of, you can safely ignore it for the time being. At the end of the meeting, or each day for a multi-day meeting, review the parking lot. You'll be surprised how many of the items will take care of themselves. Those that haven't by the end of the session are assigned to someone, and recorded on a task list for follow-up. The parking lot can also park unnecessary detail. In a CRC Card Session, I use the back of the card for a similar purpose. Someone will have been sent to the session with strict instructions: "Make sure you tell them about the new manufacturing classification we need." So at every turn, this poor guy tries to bring up this low-level detail. No problem, just write it on the back of the CRC card. He now sees it's been recorded and will shut up about it, and you *have* recorded it so won't forget it.

Now the tough part. What if a problem is both unpleasant *and* difficult? I'll leave that as a koan for the reader.

Five *Why*'s will Make You Wise

I was once browsing through a book on Systems Analysis looking for examples of problem statements when I found an example of an analyst whose boss sent him to look into a problem in Accounts Receivable. The Analyst spoke to the Receivables Manager, who indicated she needed a report of those customers who were past due on their accounts for whom there was no telephone number on the database. I turned the page expectantly, hoping to see how the analyst rooted out the cause of the problem. To my disgust, there was a problem statement: "Need a report that shows past due customers with no telephone number."

I almost threw the book across the room, because a need for a report, or screen, or even a system, is *never* an analysis problem. It may help to *solve* a problem, but it is not a problem in itself. Of course, a report (screen/system) could be giving incorrect information, thus making it a programming problem, or be poorly designed, thus making it a design problem, but the need for a bug fix is not an *analysis* problem. In the example given, the problem was "We don't have the telephone numbers for customers we need to contact because they haven't paid their bills." The analytical question is "*Why* don't we have these telephone numbers? *Why* did we lend money to people we can't contact?" Is an edit needed on the input screen to require a phone number? Are they unable to capture contact information at the logical time? Maybe it's not on the form, or in the database. Or is it captured, but later lost?

And I'm sure you've seen this example, maybe not exactly this way, but something similar. Say a sinkhole develops in the street near your home. You call the local government office in charge of roads and get a refreshingly interested response. "This is terrible, cars could be damaged, people could be hurt. Something must be done, something *will* be done." Sure enough, right away a crew shows up, and installs prominent signs: DANGER: Rough Road.

Look for what a Quality guru calls the *root cause*. You need to understand WHY the problem started, so ask *why*'s until you're wise. Now your next question is probably: How many why's do you ask? Most children figure out the why word can always be grammatically and logically used to reply to any statement. "Time for bed." *Why?* "Because you have to get up early." *Why?* "Because you have to go to school." *Why?* "So you can get a good job." *Why?* Etc., etc., etc. The only escape is the famous

Because-I'll-give-you-a-spanking-if-you-ask-why-again tactic. So I'm afraid this is one of those Zen situations, you'll know the answer when you hear it. In *Kaizen* and *Gemba Kaizen*, Masaaki Imai suggest you ask why five times, even calling the technique "Five Why's", since chances are five will uncover the root cause.

In one example, a worker is throwing sawdust on the floor. Why? Because the floor is slippery. Why? Because there is oil on it. Why? Because the machine is dripping. Why? Because there's a leak in the oil coupling. Why? Because the rubber lining is worn, and needs replacing.

In an example given by a Toyota Vice President, a machine stopped running. Why? Because an overload blew the fuse. Why? Because the bearing wasn't lubricated properly. Why? Because the pump wasn't working right. Why? Because the axle was worn out. Why? Because sludge got in it.

I've experienced this example: the report is wrong. Why? Because wrong data were entered. Why? Because the user mistyped the data. Why? Because the user was confused. Why? Because the programmer didn't understand the problem. Why? Because of incomplete analysis. Always ask yourself: "Is this a problem, or a solution, or a solution looking for a problem?" Are you attacking the problem, or just a symptom? Don't fight the fever, fight the disease causing the fever.

> **To get to the root cause,
> Ask "Why" five times.**

The Rule of Five is more or less arbitrary, but the ancient Greeks sought the quintessence, that is the fifth essence, of all things, so they seemed to agree the real answer is five levels from the apparent. When should you stop asking why? When you've gone too far. Sometimes it's only clear you have the root cause when you've gone beyond it into the realm of the child's recursive why.

Think Outside the Box ~~Great icebreaker exercise / more than one solutions~~

In many systems analysis courses, the section on modeling the current system is followed by a segment on recording the new, dramatically improved system, with lunch in between. How the brilliant new design appeared from the current design never explained, so during lunch, a miracle must have occurred to make the new solution appear. And of course the new solution was the creative part, the part you most need help with.

Many books and gurus will tell you the best way to solve a problem is to "Be Creative!" Now, why didn't *you* think of that? Perhaps you weren't creative enough to think of it. The difficulty is that you can't just write in your calendar: "Tuesday morning, 9:00-11:30: Be Creative". If you press, this advice will be made a bit more specific: "Think outside the box!" Just what box are we talking about?

The familiar connect-the-nine-dots exercise. The problem is: "Connect the nine dots by drawing a series of straight lines without lifting your pen." The twist to the problem is this: The obvious solutions require using *five* or more lines. Your task is to do it with fewer than five lines. Try a few:

HINT: A number of solutions are not obvious because of a requirement that we mentally read into the problem. Most people construct an imaginary box around the nine-dot pattern. Some people even describe the pattern as "Nine dots arranged into a box". So, you guessed it, the solution to this problem will require you to *think outside the box*. The usual solution offered is a four-line solution that involves arranging the lines such that we get an outside angle on the dots, extending the line outside the mental box we constructed around the dots. This is the famous (or infamous) box everyone is trying to get out of.

But there are actually several *one*-line solutions available to Zen analysts, and they don't even require you to go outside the box. You could use a calligraphy brush to draw a line such that a single line passes through all the dots. Another is to use origami (the Japanese art of paper folding) and fold the paper so the three rows of dots align with three dots touching at the edge. Then use a pencil to draw one line through the dots.

The point of all this is to "Think Different," and get the creative juices flowing. Some people find this exercise either entertaining or silly. But it makes a great icebreaker, and helps loosen people up, and that can allow creative thoughts to flow.

Try to discover your most creative time of day. I tend to get my best ideas in the early morning hours after I've just awakened. I usually think best if I don't turn the lights on, a problem since I can't see to write the ideas down. Since I've reached the point that I know so much that to remember anything new I need to forget something to make room for it, I keep a pad in my pocket in the day and by the bed at night, so I can scrawl down my fabulous ideas that I later can't read. I'm also working on a way to take notes in the shower but I can't reveal anything until I get the patent. But seriously, just the act of preparing to take notes can put you in the right frame of mind.

Creative people usually keep on rolling with the flow. Mick Jagger of the Rolling Stones says he never tries to compose lyrics in verse. Even though his lines must rhyme, he says rhyming as you write slows the flow and ruins it. The same is true with writing—don't try to write grammatical sentences with kurektly spellt wurds. Just let the words flow, then go back, correct any errors, and make it sing. Likewise with starting a system or writing a program—start with a small step and go from there.

And don't forget: if you take another person's idea, it's plagiarism, and despicable. But if you take two or more people's ideas, it's *research*, an admirable pursuit worthy of the true scholar you are. So steal ideas shamelessly, from books, friends, movies, plays, even the world itself.

Everybody Knows About Chicken Feed

When I was a junior economist before I got into computers, I was sent to a class on computer principles for non-technical people ("users") like myself. A tape was played of a speech that had been made by one of a pair of young men who had started a consulting firm using the power of computers in new and exciting ways. Unfortunately I've lost the reference but it's a good story that illustrates some important points even if I might not have the details right. As Ken Kesey would say, it's a true story even if it didn't happen.

They were just out of school, one with a degree in Mathematics and one in Computer Science. There is a technique in mathematics called "linear programming" that was developed in the early nineteenth century. Despite its name, it has nothing to do with computer programming, but as its name might suggest, it was ideally suited to the computer. In fact, linear programming had been considered something of an oddity. Although it was a method of solving problems involving simultaneous linear equations, and there were many applications where solving these equations would be valuable, it was so tedious and time consuming as to be impractical. And then along came the computer, which excelled at tedious and time-consuming work.

Our heroes decided to specialize in linear programming. They arranged for some computer time, worked up some programming programs (that is, computer programs to do linear programming) and found a likely application. They had studied at U.C. Davis, and so being good Aggies they not surprisingly came up with an agricultural problem. Are you ready for this? It was chicken feed. No kidding, chicken feed.

Now chicken feed might not sound too complicated to you, but in fact it is. There are literally hundreds of different commodities that can be used to make chicken feed: corn, wheat, rice, sorghum, etc. Each has a certain amount of calories, vitamins and minerals. The trick is to mix the ingredients such that the resulting feed has the right amount of each of the dozens of vitamins and minerals needed to make a happy and healthy, not to mention profitable, chicken. This problem might sound like it would have been solved years ago, but there is an independent variable, as mathematicians a wont to say: each of the hundreds of commodities that can be used has a price, and *that price is constantly changing*. So the ideal chicken feed formula literally changes every time some commodity is sold on the Chicago Board of Trade. As the price of a commodity goes up, you should use less of it. But this lowers the amount of each vitamin and mineral that commodity contains; and so you'll need to increase other commodities to make up the deficits. Surprisingly, it will be rare to simply lower the amount of one commodity and replace it with another, because the mix of nutrients is different in each. To put enough of the new commodity in to replace the nutrients that the old commodity is high in you'll inevitably wind up with an excess of whatever the new commodity is high in. Reducing this surfeit will almost always entail adjusting the level of a third, and a fourth and then a fifth commodity. I probably haven't done a very good job of explaining the complexity, but trust me, I took a course in Mathematical Economics in which we devoted much of the semester to these types of problems and they are a lot harder than they look.

So our heroes found a client to experiment with. The feed company would let them work up chicken feed formulas on approval, which is to say, if the company didn't approve of the results, they wouldn't get paid. The company's formulas were the work of a couple of wizened old men who had done this all their lives. They looked over the commodity prices each day over coffee. Most days they'd keep reading the paper and drinking coffee, but some days they'd see something that caused them to spring into furious action. If the prices called for it, they'd spend frantic hours making up a new formula. That's a chicken feed formula, not a mathematical formula, because they used no math of any kind in their decisions. It was all gut feel. Our heroes wondered why they didn't just consult the chicken entrails, since that would have been about as scientific as the method they were using. The company's problem was the formula guys were both approaching retirement age, and no successors were evident.

So, our heroes got all the USDA figures on nutrition content, and the numbers for the ideal meal for super-chicken, and set up their computer to determine the ultimate chicken feed. Some hours later (even with the best computers of the age, the calculation took a long time) the answer came back, and exceeded even their wildest expectations: they had a formula that would produce feed for *less than a quarter* of the current cost. Triumphantly, they returned to the company with their recipe.

"That will never work!" said the formula makers.

"Why not?" asked our heroes.

"Too much molasses". It seems molasses is runny, and if you put more than one or two percent in the mixture, it just runs out of the burlap bags.

"Why didn't you tell us about molasses?" our heroes asked.

"Everybody knows," they replied, "that molasses is messy".

But this was not a real setback. They simply gave their computer one more constraint, *et voila*, a few hours later, another fantastic recipe. This one saved a little less than half, but that's still pretty darn good! So, they rushed back to the company.

"That will never work!" said the formula makers.

"Why not?" asked our heroes.

"Chickens won't eat that."

"Why not?"

"The mixture will be reddish-brown in color. Chickens won't eat anything red or brown."

"What, do chickens have color fetishes?"

"No, but it will look like dirt to the chickens."

"Why didn't you tell us about colors?" our heroes asked.

"Everybody knows," they replied, "that chickens don't eat dirt."

Now this was a little more complicated, but not impossible. It took a couple of weeks, but they were able to build in the color components of each ingredient and make sure the result would appeal to even the most discriminating bird's eye. The resultant formula only saved fifteen percent or so, but that can add up to a sizable sum over the years.

"That will never work!" said the formula makers.

"Why not?" asked our heroes.

"The formula is too rich. It will cause diarrhea."

"Why didn't you tell us about richness?" our heroes asked.

"Everybody knows," they replied, "you don't want your chickens to have the runs".

And on and on. They kept reformulating, with each attempt losing more and more of the cost advantage, until they finally ran out of money and had to give up. At that stage, their best formula was within one-half of one percent of the cost of the formula the old guys had concocted using their unscientific approach. The company started a crash course to train some new feed formulators.

> **Beware of What Everybody (except you) Knows**

When you are involved in a development project of some kind, be it for a new computer system or a new way of doing a manual process, beware of what everybody (except you) knows. There is often an assumed level of knowledge. They're not being malicious (that's *another* problem), it just never occurs to them you wouldn't know. The analyst's job is to uncover the system—the users job was to make chicken feed, and they were quite good at it.

This is true both when you are trying to understand something, and when you are explaining something to someone who is unfamiliar with it. There are a lot of unspoken assumptions shared by those familiar with a process that will not be obvious to those who are not familiar with it. And remember, the human mind has an amazing tolerance for complexity and ambiguity that computers do not.

"No Fishing from Bridge"

One upon a time the fishing was excellent on a certain riverbank. Many people came to fish there, and, in time, piers were built to fish from. One day, a ferryboat company was formed to take people across the river, and quite naturally decided to dock at the existing fishing piers. Over time, the piers were enlarged, roads were built to the ferry landing, facilities were built, and the area was generally improved. As time passed, and more and more people crossed, it was decided to build a bridge. Because there were roads and land available at the ferry crossing, it was quite natural that the crossing point chosen for the bridge was the ferry landing. Soon the bridge was ready, and signs were posted: "No fishing from Bridge", which is quite ironical, since the bridge would not have been there if it had not been such a good place to fish. Not only has a great place to fish been lost, but the bridge is not in the ideal location for a crossing, either. The legacy system (fishing) caused the eventual system (the bridge) to be in the location it was, which was actually ideal for fishing, not crossing. If you don't think this fable applies to computer systems, consider how many programs today are optimized for punched cards. As I pointed out in my first book *Solving the Year 2000 Crisis*, the Y2K problem is an example of a "Good idea at the Time" leading to serious problems down the road. Take care when determining why things are as they are. It could be for a good reason, a bad reason, or no reason at all.

> **Things are the way they are**
> **For a good reason,**
> **For a bad reason, or**
> **For no reason at all**

There is a tendency to think things ought to be as they are. David Hume pointed this out as a fallacy of assuming whatever is ought to be. In history, we often assume the actual victors ought to have won: "Luckily, Hannibal was defeated, and Rome was saved." But if things had gone differently at Zama, we'd likely say, "Luckily, Scipio was defeated, and Carthage was saved." If you assume what "is" ought to be, there will never be improvement. In Hume's time, there were colonies, slaves, peonage, diseases, etc.

> **Hume's Fallacy:**
> **No ought deducible from is**

Let's consider some cases where there *was* a good reason to do something a certain way, but now that original reason is no longer valid.

If you leave a floppy in your PC the machine won't boot up, because the original PC had to boot from the floppy since it was the only drive the machine had. But now when every computer boots from the hard drive we're still stuck with that annoying protocol. An argument is made it needs to continue that way so that in the event of a hard disk crash you can still start the machine. Maybe, but couldn't the procedure look at the floppy, and if it doesn't find a system disk, go to the hard drive? And nowadays, if your hard disk crashes you'll get it fixed, not revert to the old floppy method.

The familiar QWERTY typewriter keyboard was designed to avoid the problem of the hammerlock. In a manual typewriter, a mechanical linkage connected the key to a hammer that struck an inked ribbon to imprint the letter on the paper. When a typist is typing very fast, one hammer can come up before the other is back down, and they clash, causing an annoying jam. The closer the two hammers are in the carriage the more their arcs overlap and so the more frequently they jam. The QWERTY layout was designed to separate keys that were often adjacent in English words, and so avoid this problem. The original reason is gone with the hammer, but we still have QWERTY, and probably the commands typed in on the spaceship arriving at a distant galaxy in the next millennium will use QWERTY.

Many Management Information Systems produce reams of reports that no one looks at. They track items that are no longer important, or that can be tracked better or easier through another method. When in doubt, turn them off—maybe no one will ask what happened to them.

But perhaps the most troublesome example of a straitjacket constraining progress is the legacy curse.

The Legacy Curse

Legacies are usually good, being something inherited from your rich ancestors. The legacy curse is the problems caused to a cutting-edge high-tech IS Department because its core systems are running on technology from decades ago. Usually written in Cobol, or even C, the problem with legacy systems is they are too good to throw away but not good enough to take you to a new level. The World would a better place today if Y2K had caused every computer and computer program on Earth to melt down and be completely unusable. Within a year or two, we'd have replaced all the old junk with something new and be rid of the Legacy Curse.

Legacy systems are victims of their own success. Your company has come to depend on its legacy systems, but cannot afford to replace them. For one thing, a replacement would be developed over months, but would require a similar investment to that made in the legacy system over a period of decades. But most important, the system has become critical, and so you must keep the old system running while replacing it. If you have ever had to live in your house while re-building it, you'll have some sympathy for the problem. Similarly, refitting the Oakland-San Francisco Bay Bridge will probably cost more than it will cost to build a new bridge from scratch, because we need to use it while we're working on it. In some cases, replacing a legacy system is like replacing an airplane's wings in flight.

Sometimes, the only reasonable choice is to build around the legacy. You surround, or "wrap" the old system in new technology. The design of the human brain is a wrapped legacy system: It includes a dinosaur brain. There's the reptilian portion, the legacy system, with a mammalian portion built on top of it. Redundant, and often at cross-purposes, it fails to maximize the use of the new technology—a poor design. However, the species had to stay alive while the better brain evolved, so we have both. The new technology, in fact, "surrounds" the old.

The evolution from four-legged to two-legged animals led to a poorly designed back. At every point it had to be better than the design before it; you can't say "Look, Mother Nature, to get you the best possible two-legged creature, we're going to have to suffer a minor setback for one or two million years, but in the long run you'll have a much better back to work with....". A two-legged creature has his hands free—but four-legged creatures don't have hands: to have two feet free would be of little value. The feet had to simultaneously evolve into hands: fingers and an opposable thumb. Likewise, standing up to see is of little value until sight improves. And you can't stand on two legs without a balance system (inner ear). Bringing all these pieces together took time.

And similarly, the current system might put severe limitations on any new system. The users may insist each increment is an improvement, and all features be available at the same time. But, you can usually still improve dramatically: You don't get the best possible solution, but you can usually get a workable solution. The design is better every step along the way, although you might wind up with a dinosaur brain in the center.

Brian Lamb, the World's Best Interviewer

Okay, you've been working hard on this stuff, so now I'm going to tell you to take a break and watch TV. Interviewing skills are indispensable during systems analysis. You must be able to extract sensitive information without offending. If you'd like to see a master at it, watch *Booknotes* on CSPAN sometime. It's on Sunday nights at 8:00 Eastern & Pacific (immediately after *60 Minutes*), and the more popular episodes are replayed from time to time. The host, Brian Lamb, spends an hour discussing a book on politics, history or current affairs with the author. The program is always interesting, not just for the topic of the book, and because he also discusses the process of writing, which has similarities to systems development, but especially because of Brian's interviewing style.

His style enables him to ask sensitive questions without offending the interviewee; in fact, he draws the author out, asking questions that might have evoked anger if asked by anyone else. He is able to ask questions that normally would draw a "None of your Business" and get the author to answer without the slightest hesitation or offense. "How much money did you make on it?" or "What made you think *you* could write a book on this topic?" He also usually asks about the book dedication, especially if the author has concealed the identity of the dedicatee.

If you can't catch the show, many show transcripts have been collected into the book *Booknotes: America's Finest Authors on Reading, Writing, and the Power of Ideas.*

2

THE TAO OF DESIGN

Information is a verb, not a noun.
> —Michael Dertouzos

A Design must have the Right Aspirations. Chapter 2 discusses design issues, such as of User Interfaces and data records, covering some things you should keep in mind when designing a system. We're called Systems Analysts and analysis involves breaking things down into their component parts to understand the system. But we probably should be called Systems Synthesists, since the goal of all our effort is to synthesize the pieces back together into a better system than we started with. And synergistic synthesis is what Systems Design is all about.

In this chapter we'll try to learn some techniques of design, what you would learn in my design dojo if I opened one. A *dōjō* is a place where a *way* is taught. The word Tao, pronounced halfway between "Dah-Oh" and "Dow", means *path* or *way*, and came into Japanese as *dō*. The "-do" on the end of the martial arts Jūdō, Kendō, and Aikidō are the very same *dō*, and it also appears at the end of Bushidō, the way of the warrior. The *jō* simply means place, so a martial arts sensei (teacher) will teach at a dojo. The Japanese seem to be able to elevate anything to a way, there even being Sadō, the way of Tea, as delightfully explained in Kakuzo Okakura's 1906 *The Book of Tea*. A way can be a way of life. To some Americans, computers can be a Way. Many followers of the Open Source movement treat hacking (in the original, good sense of the term) as a way. Eric S. Raymond, in *The Cathedral & The Bazaar*, recommends that you Study Zen, and/or take up martial arts, if you want to truly understand hacking. "The mental discipline seems similar in important ways."

A Protest From One of the Inmates

In his book *The Professor and the Madman*, Simon Winchester describes an incident concerning a W.C. Minor, M.D., a doctor at the Broadmoor Criminal Lunatic Asylum in England. Dr. Minor had contributed significantly to the *Oxford English Dictionary* by providing numerous citations of word usages. Imagine the OED editor's surprise when he visited the good doctor and discovered that although Dr. Minor was at the asylum and was indeed a doctor, he was not at the asylum *as* a doctor, but as an *inmate*. He had been adjudged criminally insane after committing a grisly murder.

To avoid any such confusion, let me be clear up front: I am one of the inmates Alan Cooper refers to in *The Inmates are Running the Asylum*. Subtitled *Why High-Tech Products Drive Us Crazy and How to Restore the Sanity*, Cooper finds the root of the problem to be that programmers are designing user interfaces, which he feels they have no business doing. I'll grant you some of the UI's I've seen drive me crazy, but are we programmers all that bad compared to other fields? How about automobiles? Computers have not been around as long cars, but one night after teaching a class at UCLA I drove to LAX down The 405, "the busiest freeway in the world", with no lights on. I could not for the life of me figure out how to turn on the lights in the rented Mitsubishi

Gallant. It had three or four posts protruding from the steering column, and switches everywhere. I tried twisting, pulling, pushing and clicking, all to no avail. I had a tight connection to make and so did not have the time or patience to keep playing with it.

"Computers are just too hard to use." So how about a little tech support? If you buy a new $100,000 Jaguar and come upon a tight parking space, what number do you call to get advice on how to park? Answer: there is none. Once a product becomes mature, the manufacturers cease giving advice on routine operation. And computers are now mature.

And we programmers are faulted for known bugs that go unfixed. I drive a classic Datsun 280Z, a sports car that received numerous design awards. The User Manual explains the use of the hatchback and warns: "Be careful not to bump your head on the latch when the hatchback is open." In the 20+years I've owned the car, I've bumped my head approximately 1.35 million times. Since they put the warning in the manual, they obviously knew the protruding latch was a problem, but they get design awards for their car; if it were software, the designer would be denounced.

And of course the lack of standardization drives us crazy. The same actions are done completely differently in each application, even in different versions of the same product. But what about in other fields? Very few things in life are standard. Tell me, where is the shoe department in the Nordstrom in San Francisco? Where is City Hall in Hoboken? Where is the men's room in the mall in St. Louis? And what I most want to know: where is the damned headlight switch in a Mitsubishi Gallant?

Outline or Refactor?

Stephen J. Gould, the late Harvard paleontologist who wrote many successful books on various topics, was asked in an interview how he prepared his manuscripts. The interviewer was surprised when Gould said he wrote them out in longhand. "Wouldn't it be better to use some word processing software? It's so much easier to move paragraphs around." Dr. Gould feigned confusion. "Why," he asked, "would anyone want to move paragraphs around?" He went on to explain that he devotes much time to working and re-working his outline, and that before he writes his first sentence he pretty much knows where every paragraph belongs and what it will say.

In *Life on the Screen,* on the other hand, Sherry Turkle describes her quandary with a course she took in college that required her to write a composition every three weeks, with an outline due at the end of the first week. She discovered she could only fulfill this requirement by writing the entire composition in one week, then extracting an outline, and holding the completed paper until the due date two weeks later. She describes her method as "bricolage", allowing the organization to emerge as she tinkered with ideas.

I could never be as exact as Gould in my outlining, nor as undirected as Turkle, but certainly some organizational thought should precede writing a book. If you have written a book, perhaps you're like me, constantly re-organizing and moving sentences, paragraphs, sections and entire chapters. To be honest, sometimes the chapter location for a topic is pretty arbitrary, even after a lot of thought. Sometimes it's just stuck somewhere. Writing a computer program works the same way. Ideally, we do a top down design, but if we're doing something new, the program might just evolve. Turkle also rebelled at a programming class she took in which the instructor insisted on top-down structured programming, which did not match Turkle's mental processes. My homeboy (he's from Oakland) Jack London said there were nine steps to a book. They were: Write, write, write; Revise, revise, revise; Write, write, write. Martin Fowler has written a book called *Refactoring: Improving the Design of Existing Code.* The book is needed because programs often evolve into poorly organized collections of statements, and the book gives techniques for sorting them back into order. For some programs the advice is similar to London's: Code, code, code; Refactor, refactor, refactor; Code, code, code. But, no cheating, you must do the refactoring!

The organization might not matter as much as you think. Only once in my career did I give a presentation to the CEO of a Fortune 500 company. My boss' boss' boss' boss. My two teammates and I were in the conference room about five minutes before the presentation was scheduled to start when one of us casually thumbed through the handouts of the presentation to discover the pages had some how been shuffled into the wrong order. In fact, the order was about as random as you could get. We only had five minutes, no staple puller or stapler, and about 25 copies that were wrong. So we made a command decision: we simply sorted our overheads to match the order of the handouts and gave the presentation in random order. To make a long story short, no one noticed! The presentation went just fine, we received many compliments on it, and all we asked for was approved.

Excerpts from a Status Report

Annie the Analyst

Week 1: We're off to a great start, we held a CRC session with the users and have identified 15 entities.

Week 2: Good progress this week, we discovered 9 more entities.

Week 3: We've identified attributive entities, adding 5 more entities.

Week 4: Our final review session found 3 more entities.

Week 5: Our detailed design is off to a great start. We eliminated 2 entities this week.

Week 6: We got rid of another 8 entities this week. A great week!

Week 7: Good news: We were able to cut another 3 entities this week.

These status reports illustrate how your goals change as the project proceeds. At first, you should be open to anything, the sky's the limit, and more is better. They want a printer that not only prints, but brews espresso and makes Krispy Kreme ® doughnuts? Write it down, it might be possible. But as you hone in on the task, the meaning of "goodness" changes: you now consider less, not more, progress. At some stage you must rule out the impossible. This is another of those middle way situations: to close ideas off too early is as bad as to fail to concentrate your effort later on. Project scope is shaped like a funnel, not an hourglass. Hourglasses are good for egg timers and figures, but not project scope.

Presentation Tips

One of the most important skills you'll need to get ahead after you become a systems analyst is the ability to make a presentation. You need to be able to stand before a group of people and demo your creation, teach them how to use it, and yes, even sell them on the idea of developing it in the first place. I saw an article recommending every Army Officer's personal library should contain, along with the obvious choices of Clausewitz, Sun Tzu and Keegan, a book on PowerPoint. In the new army, "We never retreat, we just re-boot!" What's true for these warriors is true of code warriors: presentation skills are an important asset to your career.

My students asked me to put together a few tips on the topic, and so you find here some more or less random observations.

Ben Franklin is supposed to have said: if you want me to speak all day, just give me five minutes to prepare. But if you want me to speak for five minutes, I'll need all day to prepare. Or the comment "Sorry to write such a long letter; I didn't have time to write a short one". Plan what you are going to say. If they ask you to talk for one hour, they probably don't mean a half hour, but they don't mean an hour and a half, either. Proper preparation will also help prevent nervousness.

> The key to avoiding nervousness is:
> Be Prepared.

Here's a piece of advice you probably won't like. If you're giving a presentation, you must get there *one full hour* before you're scheduled to speak. In fact, pretend like you are scheduled an hour earlier. Why? First, one of the secrets to a good presentation, both for your audience and your own piece of mind, is not to be nervous. If you head out early, a flat tire or traffic jam won't throw you into panic mode. If you don't know where the place is, don't worry; you can afford to get lost. It also makes it possible to recover from preparation problems. If the door's locked, the projector missing or the room arranged wrong, you can usually find someone and get it corrected, which you won't be able to do if you don't have that hour to spare. If everything's fine, you can have a cup of coffee, read a newspaper, or just explore. You'll be glad you did.

> Aim to Arrive *One Hour* early.

There are some things that should never be said in a presentation. First and foremost, never, ever say: "I know you can't read this"! How many times have you been at a presentation where an illegible slide is put up and the presenter says exactly that? Look, if you know they can't read it, fix it so they can. But if for some ridiculous reason you don't fix it, at least act surprised: "My goodness, you probably can't read that!" It's bad enough you were too disrespectful to make a readable presentation without insulting them by making it clear you intentionally allowed it to be unreadable.

> ## Never, ever say:
> ## "I know you can't read this"

And don't admit nothin'! If you make a presentation error, simply correct it. Don't accentuate the negative. Never say: "I forgot to tell you about this", just tell them. Never say: "I already told you this, but…"; if it bears repeating, repeat it; if not, don't. An especially never say: "I'm really nervous." There's a very good chance they won't notice if you don't tell them, and every time you say it, you force yourself to notice it, and make it worse.

> ## Don't admit nothin'!

Designs that Should be Flushed

Award time. What's the dumbest design in the history of the World? Not just systems, but any design. Think for a minute, then see if you agree with my answers. First, the runners up: The third Dumbest Design In History is the Caps Lock on the PC. They know it is a problem because Microsoft Word ® even has a feature to reverse the error it causes. Remove the key, or make it smaller, and put it in a less prominent place. It's not as bad as a system I saw where the help key was F2, right next to system disconnect key F1, but it's so annoying to so many people to easily beat that one out.

Now, the first runner up: The second Dumbest Design In History is: the low-flow toilet. There aren't many plumbers in Congress as far as I know, but that didn't stop Congress from designing a toilet and making it illegal to make any other. Congress passed a Law requiring low-flow toilets with no idea if they were even possible. They erred in not passing the predecessor law changing the outmoded law of physics that requires two, or sometimes three flushes to do the job in these toilets, which uses far more water than a single flush from the "water wasting" design.

So what's the dumbest design error in history? No, not the clock on the VCR that always flashes 12:00. This design wins the Dumbest-Ever Award because it's been repeated over and over and over and over again. A man can get to the moon faster than a woman can get into a restroom. Why aren't there ever enough women's restrooms? Has no architect ever gone to a play, a ball game, a concert, and seen, or stood in, the women's room line at public facilities? The feminist responds it's a reflection of the lack of woman designers, but despite feminine inroads into this formerly male-dominated profession, brand new buildings *designed by women* still have the problem! And surely even the male architects have gone to a play with a wife, mother, or friend of the opposite sex and had to wait on her?

Bad UI

Our weakness as an industry in designing interfaces can be seen in the titles of two leading books on interface design. Alan Cooper's *The Inmates are Running the Asylum* implies the present design teams belong in an asylum, and Jef Raskin's *The Humane Interface* implies our designs are so bad as to be *inhumane*!

My girlfriend worked for a law firm where one of the three partners decided to form his own office. Although he was liked and respected, many of the staff were reluctant to join him at the new office. "I'm not willing to do all that work", they said, "to set up the new equipment. Not just the computers, printers and the network, but even fax machines and telephones need to be programmed. The various machines are all different. You have to install all that software. Forget it!" And you thought computers were going to *simplify* our lives.

Consider flashing, blinking and beeping to catch the user's attention. Flashing and blinking are examples of features, like cutesy sounds, that are initially seen as cool. After a little while, they seem cute. Not much later they are annoying. Eventually they'll turn your users into axe murderers looking for the idiot that programmed the sound and light into the system. So use them with care. Forget the Netscape HTML `blink` tag, and while you're at it forget Microsoft's `marquee`. The one time it would always be appropriate to use any of these would be if you really hate the users of your system and want to punish them, or want them to leave your website and never come back.

But seriously, if you are considering attention grabbers, some ideas to consider: Use them sparingly, not for normal, routine conditions, but only for important information. In a nuclear power plant, don't use flashing red to indicate that the coffee is ready and the same flashing red to indicate there's a core meltdown that will kill every man, woman and child within 500 miles of the plant. Do you routinely call the police when you hear a car alarm? Of course not—it's 99.99% certain it's a false alarm. In other words, it should be based on level of importance and used consistently. Consistency is important both within your system and across other systems in use. And special indicators should turn off when the problem is fixed.

Overuse of any of "fail-safe" mechanisms causes the fail-safe to fail. I observed the failure of a technique due to overuse on a system. The users of the system had prepared little cards with codes:

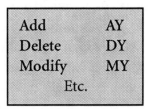

Add	AY
Delete	DY
Modify	MY
Etc.	

Every command ended with "Y". When I asked, no one knew why all the Y's. As I was playing with the system, I typed D without the Y. A little screen appeared asking

Are you sure you want to Delete this record? Y-Yes N-No

So the "Y" was actually answering a confirmation message meant to prevent errors. But since the users had to confirm even the most trivial command, they thought of the Y as part of the command and so never even saw the confirmation.

Pickpocket's Paradise

When I was installing an Accounts Payable System in Korea, one of the startup tasks was to fund the petty cash account. As you probably know, a petty cash account is intended to allow ready access to small amounts of cash to cover minor everyday expenditures for which a check would be inappropriate or inconvenient. The AP Manager, Mr. Park (anonymous enough, since 95% of all Koreans are named Park, Kim or Lee) wanted to put several million US Dollars in the fund. "Mr. Park, $1,000,000 ain't petty!" we told him. But he did have a problem and one we hadn't anticipated. Korea has a cash economy. Being an American company, we had the odd habit of paying our employees by check, but being in Korea, the company itself brought cash in on payday and cashed all the employees' checks right then and there. If you are a pickpocket, I have just one word of advice for you: "Korea"—They don't use plastic there; everyone is carrying lots of cash. So when the company had to pay a port fee or hire stevedores, they used cash for the payment, which could be substantial, so they needed to make large cash payments.

In Japan the perception is the opposite: checks are quaint. Why would you send me a piece of paper that I have to take to my bank that they send to your bank which sends the money to my bank so I can get the money? Why not just have your bank give my bank the money? When I lived in Tokyo, I paid my rent by telling my bank to deposit the correct sum in my landlord's account. So in Japan you give a list of payments to your bank instead of mailing a check to each payee. Unfortunately, I had joined the team after the design was completed, and our analysts had missed some of these differences because of cultural blinders. It never occurred to them that payments could be handled any way other than the way they were handled in the USA at that time, despite the fact that the US had once been a cash economy like Korea, and is moving toward an electronic system more like Japan.

> **Moral: Take Culture Into Account:**
> **There's More than One Logical Way to do Most Things**

Don't Over-Automate

You've probably seen something similar to the following, maybe even done something like it yourself: A document has been typed into a computer. Someone needs a copy of the document, so he gets a copy on a floppy, but it's in incompatible software, so he can't load it onto his computer. He and the author call tech support, and the three of them spend an hour and get the document successfully loaded on the computer. A happy ending? No! Even a two-finger typist (real programmers don't touch type) can type a two-page document in ten minutes. In the scenario above, three hours were spent to avoid ten minutes of work!

One time I worked on a team that had just acquired a new modeling tool and needed to convert from the old tool to the new one. While the data administrator and the lead programmer held a long, boring meeting to discuss how to use exports and APIs to convert the old model to the new, I went to my cubicle and manually entered the new model into the new tool, finishing before the now unnecessary meeting had figured out how to accomplish automatically the task I accomplished while they talked about it. Since I was new to the project, I also benefited by learning about the model in the process.

Or how about this conversation: "Isn't Barb coming to the meeting? George, you were going to tell her about the meeting." George replies, defensively: "I couldn't, Email's been down all day." Incredulously: "Uh, George, she sits at the desk next to yours! Don't you ever talk to her?" If Email is down, you can send a postcard, a memo, or leave a note on the person's desk. It wasn't that long ago that there was no Email or even voicemail, but now that we have them we can't live without them.

We technologists often see a benefit in technology for technology's own sake. When we reach the end of our analysis and design effort, we should have designed a significantly better system. If the new system doesn't change your way of doing business, don't bother. So hopefully you won't be paving the cow paths or putting disk brakes and rack-and pinion steering on the horse buggy. You should never simply automate current bad system so you can make the same mistakes more efficiently. IT should change your way of doing business.

What You Can't Give

The sci-fi classic *A Hitchhiker's Guide to the Galaxy* ends with a computer revealing the answer to the ultimate question. Alas, you will only have the data you've a place to store, and so although the computer had computed the answer to the ultimate question, the computer did not store the question, so no one knew what the question was.

> **Nēmō dat qua nōn habet.**
> **One cannot give what one does not have**

An analyst had designed a key report in a system I was working on that would be a statement summarizing the customer's activity and computing a new balance. Unfortunately, there was no place to keep the previous balance, so the calculation was not possible. Often, after a system has been designed, users will a want calculation based on uncaptured data. So think it through, make sure you have it.

p.s. No, "Nē mō dat qua nōn habet" isn't Japanese, it's Latin. Got to get some mileage out of the two years of Latin I had to take in High School (—in Japan!).

Type, Status, and Date

Type, status and date are probably the most dangerous words you'll encounter in systems design. Whenever you hear these words, you should immediately ask *what* type or status. For example, you'll surely find universal agreement that your customer database will need to track "customer type", and you'll surely reserve space for it. After you've set the database up, however, you'll discover one person's type is "small, medium or large", another meant "individual, corporate or government", still another meant "minority-owned, women-owned, or neither", etc., etc. The problem with type is usually there are several different types from several perspectives and you might miss one.

A similar problem exists with *status*. But with status, there is not usually a status missed, but several that are incorrectly combined. For example, the order status might be thought to proceed through a life cycle: open, filled, paid, closed. That's the usual sequence, but what if your customer pays in advance? In this case, you can either close it, in which case it will never be filled, or leave it open, in which case the payment is not acknowledged. In fact there need to be two independent fields: fulfillment status (taken, filled, back-ordered, or canceled) and payment status (open, paid, or overdue).

I have also encountered the missing qualifier with an invoice date. Shortly after a new multi-million dollar system was installed, the users asked us to do an analysis of how timely payments were on invoices and embarrassingly enough we were unable to do so, because despite the fact we tracked six dates on the invoice—the invoice date, the date received, the date entered, the date paid, etc.—we did not track the due date of the invoice. The analysts on the project just assumed that one of the six dates had to be the one, but sure enough, we didn't have this basic data.

Type, status, and date always need at least two qualifiers. The first will be the name of the entity, such as invoice, payment or order. But it's a mistake to stop there. There will also be another qualifier to explain what about that entity is being tracked.

> **Lesson:** *Type*, *Status*, and *Date* always need at least two qualifiers

Payment Level

Here's a quick quiz. In most businesses there is a customer who makes an order for several items. The order is usually represented by an Invoice entity, because the receivables department usually collects the payments and they deal with the invoice. Either way, the customer got some package of goods and now needs to pay for them. So the quiz: Should the payment be recorded at the Customer, the Invoice, or the Item level? Think about it carefully for a few minutes. Ready? And the answer is (drum roll): It depends! (You knew that). Any of these levels might be correct depending on how your business operates.

First the customer level. Payments at the customer level are typical of credit cards. A credit card carries a pool of debt associated with you, the customer, not with any purchase you made. Payments and charges are accumulated into the pool, called the balance, and no association is even attempted between the payments and the charges. So if, for example, you buy a book for $20 at bn.com, and CD for $20 at Borders, then make a $20 payment, American Express makes no attempt to decide whether you paid Barnes & Noble or Borders, or paid half of each. What if you went to Hawaii three years ago, and at the end of the trip your card showed a $1,000 balance? If the balance has remained $1,000 despite much activity on the card, you might argue that the trip to Hawaii has never been paid off. On the other hand, if you took a trip to the Caribbean last year, you could argue you had paid Hawaii off, and that the balance was actually attributable to the Caribbean trip you took last year, since you chose to Calypso instead of paying the debt off. I've read articles where it was claimed the US is still paying for World War II. The argument goes that during the War, the National Debt increased by billions of dollars and has never gone down. Therefore that portion of the debt should be attributed to WWII. But it's just as easy to argue that WWII was paid off long ago, and that at various times the US built a national highway system, fought wars in Korea and Viet Nam, and went to the moon, instead of paying the debt down. An accountant would say you're arguing LIFO versus FIFO. In LIFO, "Last In, First Out", each payment would be assumed to pay the most recent debt, and so WWII is still on the books. In FIFO, "First In, First Out", WWII was paid off long ago and our most recent ventures are responsible for the debt. In any event, if you track at the customer level there is no matching of payments to invoices and if that's how your company operates the correct answer to the payment level is "Customer".

Businesses that don't have a revolving credit plan might track at the invoice level. Each order is expected to be paid for, and an invoice is either mailed or included in the package with the goods. The customer usually pays the invoice in full. If he makes a partial payment the invoice remains open until the payments match the invoice total.

If the customer returns an item for credit it will work similarly to another payment and will close the invoice when the credits and debits are equal.

But it is also possible the payment should be applied at the item level, and if your business needs at the item and you have it at the invoice level it can be a real problem. I will never forget this problem because of a very embarrassing experience caused by this kind of design error. American President Lines had spent some millions developing a new receivables system that was supposed to cover the entire company and all its subsidiaries. APL owns ships for ocean freight, but also owns a rail subsidiary, originally to move the cargo from ports to inland destinations, but now carrying even domestic traffic. The subsidiary was called API, American President Intermodal—"intermodal" being the shipping industry's term for combined ocean and land transportation.

I had not joined the project until after the design was finalized, but I was now the manager and publicly responsible for the project during roll out. Right away, API developed a problem. At first we thought it was political, in that since API had had its own system, and resented big brother APL imposing anything on them, they were being overly critical, especially since the system had already been installed at many other sites without any problem. But after closer examination it turned out there was a design incompatibility. APL needed payments applied against *invoices* but API needed them applied against *items*. This was because of the chaotic nature of the rail system. You might find it hard to believe, but freight forwarders who want to ship cargo in the rail system don't reserve a boxcar, they just find an empty car and put cargo in it. The owner of the rail car then has to figure out who used the car; in many cases they guess wrong the first time and bill the wrong company. Sometimes they bill the forwarder when the actual shipper should pay, and sometimes they bill before the information has filtered through as to who actually used the car. Therefore the customer will frequently "decline" some of the items on the invoice. Since these items need to be researched to find the correct customer, it is essential that the system track payments at the item, not the invoice, level. The analysts who visited API failed to realize that the two companies operated so differently, and now we had a fully implemented database that could not meet API's most basic need. After wracking our brains long and hard we were forced to come to the politically embarrassing decision to admit we could not serve API and support their request for funding for their own system. Several hundred hours of programmer effort had been devoted to API programs and requests were scrapped. Ouch! Even though I had nothing to do with the design, I cringe to this day when I think of it.

Redundant & Superfluous

Here's an old story. John McCoy, a hatter, decided to make a new sign for his shop. And so he designed a sign with his name: "John McCoy", his profession: "Hatter", his motto: "Fine Hats Made and Sold", and a big picture of a hat.

Before going to the expense of having the sign made, he checked with several friends to get their input. He wanted to be thrifty, and the cost of the sign would depend on how much was written on it. The first friend suggested he remove the word *Hatter*: "Since it has a picture of a hat, and says 'Fine Hats Made and Sold', it's obvious you're a hatter." He asked a second friend who advised him to remove his name from the sign. "After all, people don't care who you are, they're just looking for hats. His third friend suggested removing the words 'and Sold' from the sign. "After all, you wouldn't have a sign up if you weren't selling hats." He spoke to another friend who suggested removing 'made' from the sign. "After all, the customer doesn't care where the hats are made, just that they are good hats." His next friend suggested removing 'Fine'. "After all, you'd be expected to call your own work 'fine', so no one will believe it anyway." So that leaves a sign that just says "Hats", which is obvious from the picture, and so he dropped that. In the end, the sign had no wording on it at all!

I say this is an old story because although any DBA can appreciate the sentiment, the story is attributed to Benjamin Franklin. Redundancy is very expensive, not because it uses space, but because of the Law of Unsynchronized Data. If you have identical data stored in two places in your database, you can guarantee they will not agree with each other. If you copy the data, then turn the computers off, have them surrounded by an army of security guards carrying night vision scopes, you can be sure that when you turn the computers back on the data will be different. So the only way you can keep data in sync is only have one copy of it. In *The Pragmatic Programmer*, Andrew Hunt and David Thomas espouse the DRY principle: "Don't Repeat Yourself"; you can say that again: Don't Repeat Yourself. One more time, Don't Repeat Yourself. At the risk of repeating myself: Don't Repeat Yourself.

> **Principle: DRY**
> **(Don't Repeat Yourself).**

There should be a place for every thing, and everything in its place. Don't carry redundant information without extraordinary justification.

Gates at the Gate

The story goes that Bill Gates died and was outside the Pearly Gates, speaking with Saint Peter. St. Peter said, "You know, Bill, you're pretty marginal. When we look back at your life there is some good and some bad. What I'm going to do is let you decide where you'll go."

So St. Peter takes him around Heaven. There are all these people sitting around on clouds playing harps. It looks pretty boring to Bill. They go down to Hell. There are all these people chained to desks, there are terminals in front of them, and they are furiously fixing Windows ® bugs. It's a little warm, of course, but not all that bad. Bill thinks, "This reminds me of the happiest time in my life, when I was in New Mexico founding Microsoft. It's not much hotter than that, and I love programming of any kind."

So Bill says, "Saint Pete, I want Hell." He's duly processed and sent to Hell. Except when he gets there, it's not quite what he expected. It isn't just warm, it's in flames, people are being burnt everywhere. And the terminals on the desks are all smashed so all you can do is sit there bored looking at them, you can't program.

Bill says, "Hey, something's wrong here, I need to see St. Peter." So he's sent to see St. Peter, and complains: "This is nothing like what you showed me." St. Peter says, "But Bill, of course you saw the Demo Version…"

3

THE CONSULTANT AS GURU

Matters of great concern should be treated lightly.
Matters of small concern should be treated seriously.
— Tsunetomo Yamamoto, *Hagakure*

Stage 3 on the journey to enlightenment is Right Speech, and consultants, the modern-day gurus, flourish or fail based on the Right Speech. Every Sunday afternoon, aircraft rise from runways on the East and West Coasts of the United States, each winging for the opposite coast. These planes are crammed full of modern-day gurus, each consultant voyaging to give the same advice on the same problems to similar clients in similar situations on the opposite side of the Continent. Do they wave as they pass? Why are they called in? They must offer some truth, simple yet profound, and this chapter will initiate you into some of their Truths. Chapter 3 speaks of consulting, including some guru fads and some techniques every guru needs, such as getting consensus, and getting your ideas used.

You Must Know the Answer to *Every* Question

When I thought I'd leave regular employment to be a consultant, I realized I might be asked virtually any possible question that could be asked about technological decisions. I worried that I would never be able to do that. But then I realized I needn't worry. I know the answer to every possible question that can be asked about technological alternatives. Sounds impossible, but it's not. As any successful consultant knows, the answer to *every* technology management question is: "It depends".

What is the best database system? It depends. If you're looking at a million-transaction database the answer will be different than if you are a single user on a PC. The essence of analysis is discovering the alternatives and what they depend on. What is the best application? It depends—on culture, and legacy and yes, especially politics. And you know what politics means. The word is formed from the Greek prefix *Poly-*, meaning "many", as in polygon, many sides. And *-tics* as in ticks, which are "blood-sucking insects". But seriously, politics will affect your project whether you like it or not. Just make sure it doesn't override technical reality. As Geoffrey James tells us in *The Zen of Programming*:

> **Never Base a Technical Decision on Political Issues**
> **and**
> **Never Base a Political Decision on Technical Issues**

The fact that there are no firm answers can help you proceed in the face of uncertainty. Late one night a Vice President was questioning the DBA and me as we made various attempts to fix a vexing problem that brought our DBMS down. "Do you guys know what you're doing?"

"Of course not, but we've never let that stop us before!" we both said simultaneously.

As a systems analyst you must deal with the feelings of ambiguity and uncertainty you'll encounter. My students are skeptical when I tell them that in my career, about half the time I did anything, and almost every time I did anything cool, I didn't know what I was doing at the time. We computer experts have a bag of tricks to use when we don't know what we are doing (which is most of the time), and that's what I used. The secret to systems analysis serenity is understanding that simple ignorance is not a problem, and relaxing. Trust your knowledge and intuition: Embrace contradiction, feel your way along, and blunder through.

Never Let Not Knowing What You're Doing Stop You!

Ambiguity is always present in the life of an analyst. You must be able to deal with it, give it your best shot and proceed. If the answers were clear, they wouldn't need you. Sometimes the uncertainty is caused by incomplete information, and if you can correct that do so, but often you can't. So you must embrace contradiction and use it to your advantage. Ikujiro Nonaka and Hirotaka Takeuchi point out in their HBR articles, and in *The Knowledge-Creating Company*: "Ambiguity can prove useful at times not only as a source of a new sense of direction, but also as a new source of meanings and a fresh way of thinking about things. In this respect, new knowledge is born out of chaos." They point out Japanese companies intentionally use ambiguity and fluctuation to cause "Creative Chaos". A team can be driven to a state of "zero information" where prior knowledge doesn't apply. Over time, the process begins to create its own dynamic order from ambiguity and fluctuation.

Simple ignorance is not knowing what you're doing, and is fine, in fact normal. Profound ignorance is exceedingly dangerous, sometimes deadly, however. In profound ignorance, you don't know that you don't know. That's why it's important to distinguish between what you know, and what you don't know.

> **The Only Thing Known for Certain is**
> ***Nothing* is Known for Certain.**

Getting your Expertise *Used*

There is a difference between offering your advice and getting it used. Being right doesn't mean you'll be listened to. My book on Y2K, *Solving the Year 2000 Crisis,* was about the only book published that correctly predicted Y2K would not be that big of a problem—but it was greatly outsold by books predicting TEOTWAWKI: The End of The World As We Know It.

Most of you have been frontline workers ("individual contributors"), some have led teams or projects, and all are contemplating consulting. What's the difference between a worker, a supervisor, a manager and a consultant? There is a subtle difference between these roles, highlighted by how each is properly evaluated. Workers should be evaluated on their performance. Supervisors should be evaluated based on the performance of other people, namely the people who report to them. Managers on the other hand, should be evaluated based on the performance of other people, particularly people who do *not* report to them. Users, DBA's, vendors, and myriad assorted technicians and reviewers all play a critical role in the success or failure of your project. Most of these critical players do not report to the manager in charge of the project. Yet if any of them fail, the project fails, and you fail, too. For a consultant, it's even worse—you will be evaluated based on the performance of the people you report to, to wit, them that hired you. So the higher in the chain (assuming you'll accept "higher" is the right word) the more your success is judged on influencing events despite the fact you have no formal, direct power. It's a matter of the balance between authority and responsibility.

In an ideal situation, authority and responsibility will be equal. If you have the responsibility to do a task, you need the authority to get it done. Responsibility without authority can be uncomfortable. Even worse is authority without responsibility. In this case someone interferes and requires you to do some fool thing that causes your project to fail, but then takes no responsibility for the outcome. For the consultant, Authority and Responsibility don't balance by definition, so take care. You have no formal authority but complete responsibility: it will *always* be your fault if a project you are on fails. Both perceptually, since observers will blame it on you, but also in fact, because as a consultant you're supposed to anticipate and head off failure.

Everyone might not be able to see it from your angle at first, so you might need to stand alone for a time: Sometimes everyone later agrees with what at first they thought was crazy. Many movies about juries illustrate this, one lone stubborn juror, as in *Twelve Angry Men*, eventually convincing the others they were wrong when they were initially certain the defendant was guilty. On the other hand, you must also follow the Middle Way: once you have stated your opinions eloquently, if your idea isn't accepted, it's time to shut up and do what the client wants. Remember the Golden Rule: Whoever has the Gold, makes the Rules.

Japan's Greatest Guru

No book themed on Japanese concepts would be complete without some quotes from Japan's greatest business guru. Japan's greatest guru is not some aesthete who lived in the mountains pondering his navel. Surprise: He's not even Japanese, but American! The most respected business guru in Japan is none other than W. Edwards Deming, 1900-1993, who went to Japan in the Post-World War II Occupation era and taught the Japanese about Quality. At the time, Japan was stagnant after its crushing defeat in World War II, and "Made in Japan" was synonymous with "cheap and flimsy". He conducted his first seminar in Tokyo in July 1950, just after the outbreak of the Korean War on June 25. In gurudom, timing is everything, and his timing was superb. Japan had been an industrial power before the War, but had had much of its industrial base destroyed and had not yet rebuilt. The Korean War was called by some a "Gift from the Gods" to Japan: the war in Korea brought huge orders for goods to Japanese factories, of which the president of Toyota said: "These orders were Toyota's salvation". John Dower, in *Embracing Defeat* notes: "This almost serendipiditous conjunction of desperation and opportunity enabled Deming's Japanese admirers to integrate his ideas about quality into the inaugural stages of new production cycles and new entrepreneurial ventures in ways that would have lasting consequences over the ensuing decades." So Deming taught the Japanese how to incorporate quality into an economy that was practically rebuilding from the ground up during an economic boom.

Deming is famous for his Fourteen Points, many of which are quite applicable to systems development, so we'll refer to him throughout the book, and will discuss many of the Fourteen Points. In his book, *Out of the Crisis*, he also lists some obstacles to attaining his management philosophy, several of which are also useful to the analyst. Below are some of Deming Sensei's principles in bold, with my interpretation of what they mean to systems analysts:

Hope for instant pudding. This is usually referred to in systems as "No silver bullet", after the ACM article of the same name by Frederick Brooks. You don't just "adopt Quality", "get CASE tools", "become Object Oriented", or "Install CRM" and magically solve all problems and fix everything. Fads constantly offer various purported silver bullets, most of which weren't even lead bullets, but paper bullets.

The supposition that solving problems, automation, gadgets and new machinery will transform industry. We love our technology, so sometimes we adopt technology for technology's sake. Deming points out that "computation of savings from use of a gadget (automation or robotic machinery) ought to take account of total cost, as an economist would define it. In my experience, people are seldom able to come through with figures on total cost."

Search for examples. Cookbook methodologies and benchmarking are examples of this trap. If it worked at XYZ company it will work here, or "Oh good, we have a methodology, we can all turn our brains off and stop thinking!"

Obsolescence in schools. Lifelong learning is the name of the game in systems development, and it's hard even for the schools to keep up. You will want to consider institutions like university extensions, which attempt to keep on the cutting edge. The University of California Extension courses, for example, are usually taught by practitioners current in the field, sterling examples such as your humble author, who strive to keep up with the latest developments. Most university academic courses are, well, academic, and often behind the times.

False starts. Don't join the Methodology of the Month Club. This happens when you don't stay with a new methodology long enough to realize any benefit. Some companies happily embrace the fad of the moment, and never actually recover the innovation costs of one methodology, tool or package before going on to the next.

The unmanned computer. The computer can be a curse or blessing. But you must still use your brain. Users too often accept the word of the computer as unquestionable truth, but programmers, who of all people should know better, sometimes do that, for example with CASE tools and code generators.

The supposition that it is only necessary to meet specifications. Deming cites an example of a programmer: "She learns, after she finishes the job, that she programmed very well the specifications as delivered to her, but that they were deficient. If she had only known the purpose of the program, she could have done it right for the purpose, even though the specifications were deficient." You should be able to explain why any feature makes sense from a business perspective before putting it into a system.

Inadequate testing of prototypes. 'Nuff said.

Deming is associated with Quality with a capital Q. Deming's impact is profound, not just on Japan but the entire industrial world, although a little out of favor. He is associated with Japan, which is down, but not out, so Quality is, too. With what is called "the Bubble Economy", Japan has lost some of its luster—even my bank, formerly Sanwa, has been acquired by a French bank and has lost its venerable Japanese name. Things Japanese do have a plus, though: they're part of American (or Global) pop culture now—sushi, karate, anime, etc. are all commonplace in the USA. Notice Spellchecker accepts such Japanese words as kaizen and keiretsu, indicating how many Japanese business concepts have been adopted into business English. So "Quality is dead, long live Quality!"

Kaizen

Kaizen is the Japanese word for the concept of continuous improvement. Its central tenet is that you must continuously improve your processes to keep a quality product in production. Not just because you can always get better, but because "better" is a moving target. What's Better? It depends on what quality is: McDonalds is quality to a kid, who would find a fancy restaurant unbearable. Quality is what the customer wants.

Which is faster? A jaguar, an antelope or a human? It depends on the distance. A jaguar is faster than an antelope for about five seconds. The cat will go hungry if it's not able to catch the antelope in a sort burst of a few seconds. And over a day a human is faster; that's why humans can hunt antelope and jaguar: the animals can run faster, but can't walk far-ther, than humans.

When the Bureau of Labor Statistics tracks price changes for the Consumer Price Index, it attempts to measure changes in price, not quality. They try to factor out any nominal price change attributable to quality improvement. For many years, when the retail price for a partic-ular make of automobile went up, the manufacturers explained the increase as a quality change: "This year's model is bigger than last year's!" Reasonable enough. But then came the gas crisis, and the man-ufacturers explained the subsequent price increases as quality changes: "This year's model is *smaller* than last year's!" At first blush it sounds absurd, but it actually makes sense. For many years "bigger is better" was the guiding principle, but conditions changed and "small is beauti-ful" became the new cry. Continuous improvement is necessary just to stay in the same place.

Even our management and technical techniques need *kaizen* applied to them. We must continue to strive for better ways to manage our processes or quality will deteriorate.

The BART Train in Perspective

In the San Francisco Bay Area where I live, the mass transit system is known as the Bay Area Rapid Transit System, or BART (pronounced "Bart", like the male name). Most riders refer to the system as Bart, and say things like, "Let's take Bart to the concert", or even use Bart as a verb: "I Bart to work." My girlfriend, however, always says: "Let's take *the train* to the play," or "I took *the train* into San Francisco to go shopping." To most Bay Area residents, this sounds strange, since "Bart" is almost always used to refer to the train, but Lily always says "the train".

Why would she use this uncommon nomenclature? Because she worked at BART. Only from outside does the train represent BART, and since Lily worked at the Bay Area Rapid Transit District, she and her co-workers needed to distinguish the parts from the whole. After all, if you called BART's legal department you might have spoken with Lily, and if you did, you might later quote her, saying, "BART said…." From your perspective, *Lily* could be "BART". In analysis it is always important to consider perspective. Each role, department, and even person has a perspective that must be considered when analyzing systems. For example, the Purchasing Department's requisition becomes Receiving's shipment and Payables' invoice. What to the Shipping Department is an order, to the accounting department is a receivable. The receivable represents the order to the A/R Department; it could be the same entity, except a different group of people care about it, and so it is usually a different entity. Also note that from an accounting perspective, if IOU, my liability is your asset. A worker can be an employee, or a contractor. The manager, the IRS, and HR all see this differently.

> **Try to walk in everyone's shoes**

Each analysis technique is driven by a certain perspective. So what's the best perspective? In the beginning, all computer programs were process-driven. Then along came Data Base Management Systems, and we became data-driven—for a time, it was fashionable for Data Administrators to proclaim themselves "data bigots". Just about everyone now agrees that both process and data are essential, in fact we once called our profession data processing, but how to bring both data and process into the equation? The extreme was to bring the procedures and data together into objects, and become object-driven. But even object gurus disagree on whether we should be driven by the objects: the UML object modeling technique as described by the Three Amigos, led by Ivar Jacobson, is use-case-driven, and Peter Coad has become feature-driven. So how about business rules?

USoft was business-rule-driven until it was driven out of business. Workflow brought other possibilities. The first workflow tools were document-driven, while current tools like SAP are event-driven. Of course your eventual goal is to be chauffeur-driven, but to get there you need to design the right system. And to do that you need at least two views, one on the data and one on the process.

You can usually learn more if you take several different perspectives. In modeling, you want both a data model and a process model, or both a class diagram and use cases. Looking at a situation from both the perspective of the East and West can also bring surprising results.

> **Always analyze from *at least* two angles.**

The Two Doctors

There is a story, probably apocryphal, about a doctor and a witch doctor. The doctor was bringing modern medical knowledge to a primitive village. When a young colonial administrator and the old physician arrived at the village they were surprised to find the village chief had called the villagers together to allow the two doctors (medical and witch) to enlighten the villagers in turn. The witch doctor went first.

The shaman described a disease that was obviously what we call smallpox, and explained how it was spread: the evil eye. People who have smallpox will, through no fault of their own, give you smallpox by looking at you. If you see someone with smallpox, friend or foe, get out of eyesight as quick as you can.

He described the disease we call malaria differently. It is caused by bad air at night. You should avoid swampy areas, cover up arms and legs, and close windows at sundown, to keep the bad air away.

He went on to describe a number of other diseases that plagued the area with equally preposterous explanations and precautions.

And so it was the turn of the real doctor to speak. The doctor was world-wise, having spent many years in various remote parts of the world, so what he said flabbergasted the ambitious young administrator: "Your witch doctor is very wise, listen to him. He and I have much to learn from one another, and I hope we will be working together to keep you healthy."

Afterward, the administrator excoriated the doctor. "How could you possibly allow such tripe to go unchallenged?"

"Because," said the doctor, "if you believe what the witch doctor said, you will do the right thing."

You see, smallpox is only spread by its victims. If you never come within eyesight of a smallpox victim, you will never catch it. And malaria is spread by mosquitoes that travel in the night air, and so if you avoid the "bad air" you will also avoid the mosquitoes and thus the disease. (Incidentally, "Malaria" literally means "bad air", because Europeans also once thought bad air was the cause.) And so on for each of the explanations the witch doctor had offered.

It is quite often possible to have a completely erroneous conception of how something works, and yet still be able to use it completely well. An example of an erroneous explanation is most people's understanding of a thermostat. When they come into a cold room, they turn the thermostat up full blast to heat the room as quickly as possible. In fact, the thermostat is actually an on/off switch, the heater is either on or off and the setting has no effect on how fast the room will heat up. The same is true of ovens. In this case, the user's misunderstanding does cause some extra work, since it's necessary to adjust the thermostat after the room heats up, but the cost is slight and so no real harm is done.

There was a woman whose TV would go on the blink whenever a bad word was said on television. The repairman took it to the shop and experimented with it. It turned out that exactly one hour and five minutes after it was turned on the TV would overheat and short out. It turns out the lady always turned on her TV at 10:00, and at 11:00 Divorce Court would come on, someone would say "adultery" within the first five minutes, and the TV would go on the blink.

> **You can be wrong about the question and right about the answer.**

Machiavellian Modelers

In some cases the consultant will be most successful by working indirectly. It is not always best to take the most direct route, but to harbor an Ulterior Motive. Here are some examples of the Ulterior Motive at work.

Phony Completion Dates

I once worked on a team where one of the contractors, let's call him Karl, was the darling of the managers. "He is the only one who always completes every assignment on time! Look at his status reports, every target date completed on time, like clockwork." Those of us that worked on the team with him knew this to be true. He indeed *reported* virtually every target date completed on time like clockwork. But since we had a policy of 100% testing of all programs by another programmer, each of us on the team had received Karl's work to check, on the target date, and had learned to set it aside for a week. Karl would be furiously working on the program after he had "finished" it, so you could be sure the program wouldn't run at all if you tried to test it the day he turned it over to you.

I was later promoted and became the manager of a team that included my old buddy Karl in it. As expected, his status reports always showed everything done on time. So what did I do about this? It might surprise you to hear I resisted the temptation to embarrass him. I realized the "reported as done" task actually served the project's purposes. As they say, the prospect of your death tends to focus the mind incredibly well: Karl would work furiously to complete those tasks, and if the actual work lagged the reported completion by a few days, there's not a real problem. What I decided to do was keep my own secret project plan on which I added a week to all of Karl's tasks.

Hidden Sources

In *What Do You Care What Other People Think?*, Richard Feynman relates his experiences on the commission investigating the Space Shuttle *Challenger* Incident. Shortly after he was appointed, he got a call from another commissioner, Air Force General Donald Kutyna. During the conversation about commission matters great and small, the General mentioned he had been working on a carburetor and he just wondered what effect cold would have on an O-ring, something that was in both the carburetor and the space shuttle. This started Feynman thinking: "That was all he had to tell me. It was a clue for which I got a lot of credit later, but it was his observation. A professor of theoretical physics always has to be told what to look for."

As you probably know, the tragedy was caused by cold temperature leading to the catastrophic failure of an O-ring. Feynman spends the next eighty pages of the book entertaining us with how this chance insight led to the discovery of the cause of the accident. And then he reveals that he later discovered that General Kutyna had in fact known there was a serious problem with the O-rings all along, because a friend inside NASA had tipped him off. The General's dilemma was how to get this critical information out without jeopardizing his friend. "His solution was to get the professor excited about it, and his plan worked perfectly." Machiavellian? Yes. But it worked.

If You Would Eschew the Subjunctive

Everyone in sales knows this one. When you're trying to persuade, get out of the subjunctive and into the active! The subjunctive voice is used to express things that might ("If I were a Rich Man") happen, while the active voice expresses what will happen ("When I am a Rich Man"). If you want something to happen, speak about as if it already has. Assume you're vying for a consulting gig. Don't keep saying "I would do such and such if I get the job", say "I *will* do such and such". Sometimes this sounds presumptuous, so be careful. But if once the client slips into active voice, switch into the active voice and talk as if you already have the job.

Brainstorming Ulterior Motives

Sometimes, you need to look beyond the purpose of the immediate task. An example of using brainstorming for an ulterior purpose is demonstrated by two contrasting approaches to brainstorming. It is not always true that the best way to do a job is to do each part in the most efficient way. I generally prefer a brainstorming session to be a wide-ranging free-for-all. Everyone should yell out their ideas spontaneously, and let the creativity flow. I measure my success in teaching brainstorming by the number of complaints I get from neighboring classrooms: they hear noise, I hear learning.

My friend and co-author Alec Sharp prefers the more structured round robin method. He has each person take two to five minutes to think silently about ideas, i.e. to internally brainstorm. He then goes around the table having each person present a new idea in turn. It's okay to "Pass"; especially after you've gone around a few times some people will run out while others still have ideas to present. He agrees with me his method is not as spontaneous, and probably doesn't encourage the most innovative thinking. Why does he do it then? Because his goal is to get everyone involved, especially the first few times with a given group. It also helps him get to know the members of the group. So he looks beyond the immediate—brainstorm a list—to the long-term—a smoothly functioning group.

Consensus

Understanding consensus is key to consulting: What it is; when you want it; and when you have it. Consensus is a part of "Japanese Management", or *Theory Z*, in the title of William Ouchi's book. Consensus is desirable when you want a sense of involvement and need commitment from those involved. Consensus is achieved when each group member can honestly say to everyone else:

> **Consensus is achieved when each can say to every:**
>
> 1. I believe that you understand my point of view.
> 2. I believe that I understand your point of view.
> 3. I will support the decision, even though it is not my first choice.

First, everyone must feel he had a chance to express and discuss his concerns, and that he was given a fair hearing, so they can say "Whether or not I prefer this decision, I will support it, because it was arrived at in an open and fair manner". As with all business meetings, it should be understood that "Silence is Assent". If you don't object to a decision, you are indicating agreement with the decision, without the necessity of formally polling the jury.

> **A Rule for All Business Meetings**
> **Silence is Assent**
> **If you don't Agree, Say So!**

Second, each person feels he can support the decision, even if it is not his first choice. Sometimes the word is misspelled as "Con*c*ensus", with a 'C' instead of an 'S'. This highlights a common misunderstanding. Consensus's cognate is *Consent*, not *Census*, so all are giving *consent* to the project, not voting on their favorite choices. They are saying: "I can live with this choice".

Knowing when *not* to seek consensus is as important as when to seek it. Consensus is not appropriate when there is a single answer; for example, don't seek consensus on whether or not a file can be transmitted over a network in less than one minute. That's a case where a test is in order, or seek expert opinion if a test isn't possible. Consensus would be appropriate as to how fast a transmittal must be to satisfy the users. If you want commitment and coordination, seek consensus, but remember it is slower than other methods.

> **To Gain Commitment, seek Consensus**
> **If there is One True Answer, get Expert Opinion**
> **If you need it Fast, Appoint a Dictator**

Conspicuous Consumption

Watch out for appearances. I had an enlightening experience with a consultant working for me. He very generously invited me and several other employees to lunch at an expensive restaurant, ordered us an expensive wine, and tipped the waitress lavishly. But since he was from out of town, we were paying his travel expenses, and, yes, you guessed it, the lunch bill was attached to his invoice with a claim for reimbursement! I certainly lost respect for him because of this incident, and he was never used again. There were other factors affecting that decision, but this incident was definitely floating in my subconscious when I needed another consultant.

Compare this with this experience. I was once on a consulting assignment when I nearly blundered at the car rental kiosk. It happened they were running short of economy cars, so they offered me, at no additional charge, a beautiful red convertible instead of the economy car I had ordered. I almost accepted, and then realized how bad this would look. Since I was traveling, my travel expenses were paid by the client, so when they saw me in that car they would think I was taking *them* for a ride.

On another occasion, appearances didn't matter. I gave some Y2K seminars in the LA area to the general public, under the auspices of City National Bank—if customers of "the Bank of the Stars" can be called "general". City National's milieu is demonstrated by the accommodations I was provided as one of their visiting vendors. They provided me with one of the cheapest rooms they had in their booking system: a suite in the Beverly-Wilshire Hotel (think of the movie *Pretty Woman*) in Beverly Hills with a balcony overlooking the pool! The suite naturally was equipped with a fax machine, in case I needed to do any movie deals while enjoying the view. Consulting does have its rewards, and in this case accepting them was fully consistent with the client's corporate culture.

4

THE WAY OF BUSINESS

Real artists ship.

—Steve Jobs

as quoted by Steven Levy in *Insanely Great.*

Business requires you to take the Right Action, so in Chapter 4 we look at the business aspects of systems, including management actions such as plans and measures, but especially, strategy. Yes, Virginia, you need to develop a little sense of business strategy. When asked at a social event: "What business are you in?" Most of us in IT will answer "Information Systems", or "Computers", or "The Software Industry" despite the fact few of us actually work for a computer or software company. According to the Department of Commerce, we're not in the software industry, we're in the industry that our employer is in. One problem with techies is we don't always know or even think about the business itself. Any technician moving to a new company will know what version of Oracle is installed, how many T3 lines there are, or what the network architecture looks like, long before learning what the corporate objectives are for the next year, or investigating what makes his user counterpart tick. Your company is out to make money, or if not a profit maker, to retain as much as possible. Yes, it's filthy lucre, but hey, that's life, and why they hired you.

The Strategy of Musashi

Musashi Miyamoto (1584-1645) was one of Japan's greatest strategists. Although he was actually a master of Kendo, the Way of the Sword, *Time* Magazine called him "Japan's answer to the Harvard MBA!" *Time* went on to say: "On Wall Street, when Musashi talks, people listen." In *Go Rin no Sho, The Book of Five Rings*—actually a letter to his sword fighting students written shortly before his death—the Sword Master enumerates nine principles of strategy. These precepts have surprisingly broad application to systems analysis, so Musashi is referred to throughout this book. Here they are, mostly Victor Harris' translation of the Japanese, and my interpretation of their applicability to Systems Analysis:

1. **Do not think dishonestly.** Notice it says do not *think* dishonestly. In Systems Analysis, it is bad policy to fool others, but it's even more foolish to fool yourself. In *Rapid Development*, Steve McConnell elaborates 36 classic mistakes in software development, lucky 13 being "Wishful Thinking", as in "The schedule is impossible but if we work hard we can make it"; or "We haven't coordinated the interfaces but we are good communicators so it will be easy"; or "No need to ask the users because we know what they want". Overly optimistic schedules are a way of life in systems (McConnell's classic mistake number 14), as is the persistent belief, despite all evidence to the contrary, that you'll make up your schedule slippage in the next phase (number 26), or that your new tool or method will save plenty of time (number 34).

2. **The Way is in training.** Being a systems analyst requires lifelong learning. Technology is changing at an ever more rapid pace; if you

don't believe me, just go into a bookstore in late spring or early summer and see how many computer books already claim copyrights for the coming year! Read a book, or better take a course from me at UC Berkeley Extension.

3. **Become acquainted with every art.** You have to understand the world to understand any system. If you are naturally interested in a variety of arts, you'll enjoy the work of a systems analysis, since broad curiosity is almost essential to succeed. To help the accounting department, for example, you'll need to understand the art of accounting. Curiosity killed the cat but is good for the systems analyst. Always strive to be eclectic, picking the best from any art. You'll notice in this book I've been eclectic. Okay, okay, so maybe random is a better word for me, but you get the idea: you should open your mind, and bring ideas and analogies from other disciplines.

4. **Know the Ways of all professions.** To help your users, you need to understand something about what they do. Computers now touch on every field, but as I keep telling you, you need to understand both business and technology to be a Systems Analyst.

5. **Understand profit and loss.** Understand Economics. (My observation has been that, as a group, Economics majors make the best systems analysts, but since I am part of that august group, I would understand if you discounted that observation.) Money makes the World go around, and also systems. Most computer systems are *business* systems, and so must cover their costs and have a favorable ROI (Return on Investment).

6. **Develop intuitive judgment and understanding for everything.** Go with the flow, your gut intuition, or *hara*. About the only way to achieve this is through experience: Good judgment comes from experience. Unfortunately, experience comes from bad judgment.

7. **See those things which cannot be seen.** At one level, that's all we do: we certainly cannot see any of the computer's electron-level activities. But as analysts, we can use models and other tools to see the unseen. See

Chapter 8 for more on this topic.

8. **Pay attention even to trifles.** The devil is in the details. All analysts know how a trivial piece of information can change everything. The trick, of course, is knowing which trifles will become important later. I've also seen this principle punctuated: "Pay attention! Even to trifles", for those of you who don't pay attention.

9. **Do nothing which is of no use.** Efficiency, economy and no redundancy. Constantly reflecting on your own techniques and improving them (kaizen) will help you follow this dictum. But also be sure the system itself, not just your development methods used to create it, follow this rule. Featuritis, where we add features for no conceivable end except the feature itself is an example of a failure to observe this principle.

How Business and Information Systems Relate

The Technical and the Business must come together: We must reconcile the irreconcilable, because business and systems are now inseparable. This can be difficult given our modern organization. Few people nowadays are actually involved in the direct production of the goods or services their companies are in business to produce. In 1776, the year Adam Smith's *The Wealth of Nations* appeared, most people working for a pin company were involved in making pins, and most people at a shipping company had something to do with ships. Today, pin and ship companies employ many more computer programmers, lawyers and accountants than pin-makers or sailors, and more executives than sea captains. As a consequence, it is easy to lose sight of where our tasks fit in the process.

In order to truly understand the relationship between systems and the businesses they support we need to break the business itself into its components. Some models represent three or five levels; that is valid depending on what you're goal is. In this model we've decided to err on the side of overkill and look at nine levels. We'll consider each tier in turn.

    I. The World
        1. The Real World
        2. The Business Model
        3. The Business Workflow
    II. Software
        4. Analysis Models
        5. The User Interface
        6. Application Logic
    III. Hardware
        7. Data Organization
        8. Machine Representation
        9. Circuits

I. Business

You were hired to create a system for your business. Your system needs to support the work of that business. I use the term "business" but of course whatever your company or organization does—be it a corporation, a government, school, or nonprofit—is the business you need to reflect in your model and thus your system.

1. The Real World. There is a real world with sunshine and rain, laughter and tears, beauty and horror, and someday it will all end. But in the meantime we need to develop systems that work in that real world.

2. The Business Model. The business model describes what the business actually does. Some companies make a formal statement of their model as a Mission Statement, but whether stated explicitly or not, every organization exists to do some things and not others. The mission, goals and objectives of the business identify a market and a product or service within that market. Whether or not formally defined, there *is* a business model.

3. **Business Workflow.** The business is supported by business processes that do the work. The business processes, whether manual or automated, standardized or informal, are a flow of work through the organization. Basically, they do the work: fulfill, or sell, or assemble, or paint, or educate. You could write an entire book on this layer alone—come to think of it, Alec Sharp and I did! See our book *Workflow Modeling: Tools for Process Improvement and Application Development* for deep enlightenment on this technique. In it we also look at five of these nine levels in greater detail, using a five-tier model that collapses the machine level.

II. Software

Most technical people are good at this level, but do not make the connection between it and the business level above it. I've broken software into analysis and programming, or application logic, because many of my readers are in this field, and this is a distinction they make, and is even a job path for them. An analysis model is an analogy to understand the structure of data which is in fact not structured at all, but a series of magnetic blips in ferrous oxide.

4. **Analysis Model.** This model represents the business. ERDs, class diagrams, etc. Could also be a design, planning, conceptual, etc. Data, process, object. Workflow. What this book is about.

5. **User Interface,** or Presentation. Automated applications need a way to present data to the humans using the system. This presentation layer is a way for humans to communicate with the machines. It includes any mechanisms by which people or other systems interact with a computer system. They are usually screens, reports, or GUI's (Graphical Use Interfaces—computer dialog screens), running on the desktop, but they could be just about anything: EDI—Electronic Data Interface between companies, a kiosk, Email, the World Wide Web, VR (Voice Recognition), computerized mind reading, or whatever new device technology might hatch next. Use Cases fall here as a model of

the interaction. Notice more and more the output of one machine is presented to another machine, and the interface can be to not an eye, but an API.

6. **Application Logic.** Application process logic ties the presentation and the data together in computer programs, turning the business rules into algorithms to properly process the inputs into outputs. They could be contained in stored procedures or application logic distributed across server or client machines, but they are usually in computer programs.

III. Hardware

This is the engineering or architecture level. Strangely, this is the most abstract, yet most reliable. In truth there is no real structure, just seemingly random bits and bytes. But since our system software provides discipline, it is the most reliable level. Unless you are a systems specialist, you never even consider this level and are largely unaware it even exists, except on those rare occasions when the hardware or systems fail, in which case you are painfully aware that there is reality behind the magic.

7. **Data Organization.** Computers don't compute: Despite the name, most computers actually do very little computing. Their major power is the ability to store and retrieve data. This is where data management and databases come in: they keep the data needed for the business to operate. Databases maintain records of people, places, things, and events affecting the business. Nowadays, they are usually saved in a relational DBMS—Data Base Management System—running on one or more servers. I include the DBMS here even though it's at root a mostly software; the DBA's who are responsible for the DBMS are usually not in the same organization as the applications programmers and systems analysts who develop the software but with the systems people responsible for hardware. Just in case they object, I've put them here as a compliment to the fact DBMS's are as

reliable as hardware, and much less subject to the problems of other software.

8. **Machine Representation.** Here we are "Close to the Machine". No structure, no relationships, data is linear (actually, usually circular, since disks spin). The machine actually models data, since it's bits and bytes and electronic blips. For example, the number 999,999 is represented 11110100001000111111, as spots that are, or aren't, magnetized on the disk.

9. **Circuits.** Electrons, gates, Integrated Circuits. I still find it astounding when a piece of sand adds 2 and 2 and gets 4! At least until we have Quantum Computing. If the *Tao of Physics* is correct, this is reality; the top level we called the Real World is the illusion, and thus we circle back.

A Business Quiz

This is not a quiz about business in general, it's a quiz about *your* business. Answer the following questions about your company (not the IT department). If you don't know the answer, write "I don't know".

1. What industry are you in? Hint: The answer is *not* IT, unless you work for a computer service firm.

2. Where does your company rank in the industry in sales?

3. Where does your company rank in the industry in use of technology?

4. What was your company's profit last year, on what revenue? Or for a government or non-profit agency, what was the total budget?

5. Are revenue, profit and/or budget increasing, decreasing or staying about the same?

6. What are your company's major objectives at this time?

7. Who are your company's competitors?

8. How has technology affected your industry in the past three to five years?

9. How will technology affect your industry in the next three to five years?

10. Is your business cyclical, counter cyclical, or relatively stable?

For any you wrote, "I don't know": Go and find out!

The Planning Paradox

Companies that plan are more successful than those that don't. But companies that actually *follow* their plans are <u>less</u> successful than those that do not follow their plan. So, should you spend months building a plan and then just ignore it??? Not exactly. You need a plan as an indicator of your course, but you must not rigidly adhere to some plan you wrote months before with incomplete knowledge. If you had a plan to drive to some distant city, but insisted on following the planned route even after you discovered a bridge was out, you'd be considered crazy. But some plans (and don't forget, a budget is a kind of plan) are considered sacred text, never to be questioned once approved. You need the flexibility to steer the best course at a given time. As Eisenhower pointed out: the plan is worth nothing, but the planning is everything.

> **Make a plan, but don't plan to follow it:**
> **You gotta be Flexible**

Target Unknown

Once upon a time, there was a small wooded han (feudal realm) whose daimyo (great lord) enjoyed hunting. One day the daimyo went hunting in a remote corner of his han, and was surprised to discover a strange sight. Mile after mile, the trees had targets painted on them, and in the bull's eye was an arrow, dead center. Although annoyed at the effrontery to his trees, the daimyo realized this must be the work of perhaps the greatest archer in the world! So he sent his samurai on the task: "Find this incredible archer!" To make a long story short, one of his samurai soon announced he had found the archer, and introduced a young lady of perhaps nine years old. This seemed unlikely to the daimyo, so he asked the girl how she had achieved such accuracy. "It's really quite easy, your majesty," she said. "First you shoot the arrow, then you paint the target."

Despite the importance of having a plan, and mapping out your future, sometimes you don't know where you are going, and that can be a good thing. Especially with new technology, it is sometimes hard to predict the outcome, but without the experiment, you'll never find the good. Allow yourself to occasionally shoot an arrow then choose the target.

Bottom-up or Top-down Planning

How should you develop your plan, then? There are two main ways, top-down and bottom-up. In *top-down* planning, you take a broad view of the IS needs of the entire organization before selecting projects. The advantages of top-down planning are clear in the view of most theoreticians: Broader perspective, improved integration, improved management support, and better understanding. If you don't have an overall plan, you're likely to wind up with a stovepipe system, with incompatible systems that don't talk to each other.

To do top-down planning, you start with a project that produces the plan. It's customary to first inventory your current systems and assess the current situation, looking for gaps in systems, technology and personnel (staff and training). Next you'll want to blueprint the ideal future situation, including database and systems, technology and staff. Then lay out a tentative schedule or prioritizing of projects. Methodologies such as IBM's ISP (Information System Planning) or Information Engineering's Business System Plan can be followed, but they are a little too formal for my tastes.

In *bottom-up* planning, you respond to business problems and opportunities. You let project proposals bubble up from the bottom of the org chart where the work is being done. Ideally, you'll set up some review and estimating procedures so top management can periodically (say annually or semi-annually) review current proposals and select projects for development. This is often faster and less costly than a major planning effort, and identifies the most pressing problems. Although it might produce less management support, it produces more line support. This can be more democratic, but can degenerate into an ad hoc-racy, worse than no plan. It fails to view the entire organization, which can lead to redundancy, and systems that are hard to integrate. You will also face the squeaky-wheel syndrome, where the loudest or most politically astute get their projects approved over more important projects, and short-term fixes are favored over strategic development. So why do more companies use bottom-up planning in practice, since top-down seems to have the edge? Top-down planning takes time up front. ISP projects can take six months to a year, and often deliver no direct benefit for several years after that. In a rapidly changing business environment plans are obsolete before they are written. So a good plan today might be better than a perfect plan tomorrow, but that's not the same as having no plan.

The ideal planning method will use *both* techniques. Nonaka & Takeuchi point out in *The Knowledge-Creating Company* that Japanese companies often use a third way called "middle-up-down". A general, overall plan should be prepared, but you must be prepared to allow the plan to change from the bottom up as well. And you must be flexible because of the planning paradox. Use both ends against the middle. If top down doesn't work, try bottom up, or even middle out. Remember there are many ways to the mountaintop.

Bugs & Quality Control

When I was in the fifth grade, I delighted in observing the many varieties of insects that inhabited the streams and fields near my home, so I decided to be an entomologist when I grew up. This was a momentous decision indeed, since it required abandoning my long-held (since early fourth grade) plan to be a Nobel-Prize-winning chemist. But when I read that chemical companies were the largest employers of entomologists, I decided my two passions were complementary—I would be an entomologist for a chemical company. It was some months before the awful realization struck. The tie between chemistry and entomology is insecticides, and the career goal of most entomologists is to kill as many insects as possible. As a consequence, I abandoned my plans for both chemistry and entomology, but eventually found a career that involved ruthlessly exterminating bugs without harming any insects—computer programming. And tracking down computer bugs is something programmers spend a lot of time doing. Why don't we get them all?

Cockroaches have been a scourge of mankind for centuries. They're actually quite easy to kill—you can step on them, poison them, throw things at them, etc. We don't because there are so darn many of them, and they are hard to find. That's exactly what we are facing with debugging: Each bug is simple to fix once you find it, but there are so darn many of them, and they are hard to find. The Yanomamo Indians of the Brazilian rainforest get terrible infestations of cockroaches. Every couple of years they completely exterminate all the cockroaches. It's quite simple: they burn all the buildings in the village to the ground, and start over. With computer bugs, you should avoid the Yanomamo solution and not burn your company to the ground in order to save it from relatively harmless bugs, just get the software good enough.

Ed Yourdon discusses the concept of "Good Enough Software" in his book, *The Rise and Resurrection of the American Programmer*. He attributes some of Microsoft's paradoxical success to this concept—they sell software with thousands of known bugs, yet are extremely successful where it counts, in the marketplace. The only logical conclusion is that the ultimate judge of quality, the consumer, has decided the Computer Scientist's definition of quality, absence of bugs, is not the measure, or at least not the full measure, of quality.

With Microsoft, it's a pure business decision. Steve Ballmer of Microsoft was said to have been asked why Windows® has so many known bugs. Why don't they just spend a little time and clean them up? Steve was reported to have replied something to the effect: "You know, for a couple of million dollars we could clean up all those bugs, and that amount of money wouldn't impact our bottom line noticeably. But if I were budgeting that money, I'd put it in advertising, not fixing bugs. Because fixing every known bug would not sell even one more copy of Windows®, and the advertising would."

Quality control is another example of finding the Middle Way. I'm going to tell you to increase quality but then just get "good enough". The term "quality control" has become synonymous with the term "quality assurance", but originally the terms were quite different. Quality *control* emphasized the word "control", not the word "quality". Daniel J. Boorstin points out in *The Americans: The Democratic Experience* that the American system of manufacturing produced a new way of thinking about "quality": Make the product as good as it needs to be, but no better, with emphasis on "no better". For example, a chain of clothing stores that produces cheap but fashionable clothes that wear out quickly might be thought to have poor quality control. This would be wrong: they probably have excellent quality control. They've decided to produce products that go out of fashion quickly, and so durability is not a concern. In fact, it's Quality Control's job to make sure they continue to produce cheap, fashionable clothing, and not slip into the trap of producing expensive, fashionable clothing by making costly improvements in durability. Quality control might also dictate removing jewels from a watch. If the jewels will cause the friction point to survive one hundred years, but the mainspring will break in ten, the additional cost of the jewels merely raises the consumer's cost with no real benefit. Quality is judged by how well the product fills its function.

An example of how "good enough" programming is employed is when credit card companies calculate due dates as a certain number of days from the billing date without regard for weekends and holidays. Note on your credit card bills how often the due date falls on a non-workday. Often there is a hidden or unannounced grace period, which functions by announcing a due date on the bill that is several days before the actual due date as calculated for penalties. This grace period allows what is essentially a fuzzy calculation of due dates to work.

In designing computer systems, you need to consider this concept of good enough. Ask, "What is the underlying purpose of this process, and will lack of this feature totally negate that purpose?" If not, it might be "good enough". Deming calls the fanatical search for perfection the "Fallacy of Zero Defects". You will never achieve that goal, so at some point you need to release the system and move on to the next one.

The Terrible Twins

The twin schedule busters are these two: Analysis paralysis and scope creep. Which is worse? That's hard to say, because like many twins, they usually travel together, and are a manifestation of an unclear vision of where you are going.

Analysis Paralysis

Beware Analysis Paralysis. It's when you study and study, and never actually do anything. If after a year you have lots of circles and boxes and arrows but no system, you have a case of analysis paralysis.

Say you need some new software. If you spend a couple of months making sure to get the very best tool, and it's only marginally better than the competition, you've wasted two months. This is similar to buying a PC: are you waiting for the prices to come down? You have a horizon effect: there's always something just over the horizon: you know in a few months there'll be a better, faster, cheaper PC out. But at some point you have to go ahead and buy one, otherwise you'll lose all the potential benefit. There's always something you don't know, something more to do, but at some point it's time to move on.

When you set out to model, your purpose is to understand or illustrate, not build the Winchester Mystery Model. Sarah Winchester's famous home, the Winchester Mystery House, is located in San José, California. Sarah, the heir to the Winchester Arms fortune, was told by a fortune-teller she would live only as long as it would take to finish building her house. So she decided to continue to build her house forever. She was the original 24x7 shop in Silicon Valley: twenty-four hours a day, seven days a week, someone was building something onto her house: stairways to nowhere, windows with a view of the wall, doors that led into empty space. Some analysts seem to have a similar goal in modeling—never finish! Unlike Sarah, who was sure she'd meet her fate if she stopped building, you will surely meet a terrible fate if you *don't* stop analyzing—your project will be cancelled and you'll never get to work on the new system! Once you *understand* the current system, you have completed the modeling, and it's time to stop and produce a system.

Scope Creep

The second terrible twin is Scope Creep. Many errors arise in drawing project boundaries, but the most common, and deadly to your schedule, is scope creep. Boundaries often become too large through scope creep—your project grows to unmanageable proportions one small piece at a time, until it's so large that forward progress is impossible, and the completion date moves further away, not closer, with each passing week. This in turn is often caused by a project scope that is actually a function or department that plays a role in many processes. When the project team starts following workflows that cross the boundaries (they will, because processes do!) it's natural to start adding activities to the scope.

Poor analysis can lead to missing an essential item that has to be added later. Or a great idea comes along, too good to leave out. You can also catch the dreaded Featuritis disease, where features are added endlessly for their own sake.

Scope is clearer if you also identify related processes that are outside your scope, and depict these early and often, and graphically. This technique also makes identifying processes easier in the first place. Simply naming a process is inadequate for people to understand what's inside and what's outside of its boundaries. The greatest protection is to clarify and communicate scope, then stick to it: just say no. Require a substitution, not an addition, when something essential is added.

Personal Objectives

I once got three annual reviews on the same day, because my boss was two years behind. This had a certain advantage, because the rating was largely based on how well I met my objectives, and since I didn't have to even set the objectives until after all three periods were over, I naturally met them all! What factors can prevent you from meeting your objectives? Naturally, I have little personal experience to draw on, since I *always* reach my objectives (ha!).

The trivial answer is "Setting the wrong objectives". In a sense, if you set an objective and fail to meet it, the objective was too difficult, or wasn't important enough to devote sufficient resources to. Since objectives are goals set and sought, you might have set unattainable objectives. This is sometimes caused by being the boy who can't say "no", a desire to make your user happy by agreeing to the impossible. This brings up a philosophical and management problem. You can always reach your goals if you set them low enough. I once had a programmer working for me who never met his goals, and one who always would. The one who always missed was one of the best programmers I ever knew, the one who made his goals was one of the worst. How can that be? Tom would promise something in a week, but take two. Why was that so good? Because any other programmer would have taken four weeks. The programmer who always met his goals would have set an objective to complete that same assignment in eight weeks, and probably beat his objectives by completing it in seven. Tom[*] needed a real challenge, so he'd constantly aim for the stars. He usually "only" made the moon, or perhaps the outer planets, but that was pretty amazing. Is the goal to make better estimators, or make better systems? If a programmer's good at everything except estimating, is he bad?

Measuring

Largely because of differences in the way testing is defined, Boris Beizer, in *Software Testing Techniques* attributes some of the wide differences in estimates to "Creative Accounting". Most programmers are creative accountants. For example "Analysis is over when the time runs out". Since analysis products are less demonstrable, it's possible to declare the analysis over whenever it is expected to be done. Then they put their heads down and program, and when forced to finally turn in their time sheets they guesstimate the hours they spent in each activity. Part of the programmer's development time is spent in unit testing, and this is usually counted in the testing figures. In many cases, testing is an integral part of the programming process and so should not be counted as part of testing. In fact, the best computer programmers intertwine

---

[*] Sadly, Tom was a victim of the AIDS epidemic.

unit testing with coding so intimately as to be indistinguishable. Testing and debugging statements are coded as part of the logic coding and the overall testing strategy partially shapes the structure of the program. This testing is, or should be, part of the programming process and is problematical to account for separately. In fact, a programming manager can usually gain instant gratification by changing the allocation of time between programming and testing. Just tell a programmer "You aren't spending enough time testing" based on the time sheet and you can be sure next week the time sheet will show more time testing. Nothing else will have changed, of course, just the number of hours *reported* on the time sheet.

There are also differences as to what is included in system testing. In traditional "waterfall" projects, the system is developed to a certain stage, and then the testers are called in and the "testing and debugging" phase begins. All work after that point is generally counted as part of testing. Inevitably some of the development work that was not finished in the earlier phase will spill over the waterfall into this phase and be counted here. And some of it is inevitably spent building new functionality identified in the testing phase. Had this new functionality been identified earlier, it would have been done, and counted, as part of programming, not testing. This method of time accounting also has the unfortunate effect of causing more time to be attributed to testing when testers become involved earlier, as by definition, the testing phase begins when the testers start testing. In the best practice scenario, testers would be involved in the project from the beginning, and so all development time would be part of the testing phase. So if you are in charge of a project you'll need Zen in addition to status reports to discover the true state of the project. Take care to illicit honesty in reporting and don't push the team into creative accounting where everything is right on track until time for implementation when you discover you're weeks behind.

What's Success?: Mallory vs. Hillary

We know there are many ways to the mountaintop. Unfortunately there are many more fruitless than fruitful ways. George Mallory famously said, when asked why he wanted to climb Mt. Everest: "Because it is there!" It's still there, and so is he. Mallory never returned from his quest, and his body lies on its slopes to this day. He was last seen alive on June 8, 1924 climbing toward the summit into the clouds with his companion Andrew Irvine, and it is an open question whether he reached the summit.

On May 29,1953, Sir Edmund Hillary, accompanied by a Sherpa, Tenzing Norgay, reached the top. Which leads to the debate: was Mallory or Hillary the first to successfully climb Mt. Everest? Mallory's advocates have argued his skills and psyche indicate he would have made it, and have scoured the slopes for clues, attempting to find any scrap of evidence in his favor.

The debate is silly. Hillary was the first to successfully climb Everest. Because in my book, by any measure, if you die in the process, you don't have a successful climb! Any endeavor that kills you is a failure, end of discussion!

> **If You Die on the Way down from the Mountaintop, It's not a Successful Climb.**

The dot.com bombs are an excellent example of not grasping this principle. If you end with a bankrupt company, a ruined marriage, or a destroyed career, you didn't succeed no matter how well you did technically. By the way, if you find yourself on the project from hell, you might want to read *Into Thin Air* by Jon Krakauer. It's an account of a disastrous attempt to climb Mount Everest in March 1996; a number of the climbers who reached the summit died on the mountain that night.

There are some real lessons on poor planning, letting objectives become overpowering, and generally how things can go wrong. You'll think your project isn't so bad, after all.

5

THE ZEN OF ECONOMICS

Economic Progress requires "Creative Destruction"
—Joseph Schumpeter

Economics is about the Right Livelihood. In Chapter 5, we look at the economic aspects of systems, taking some principles from the Dismal Science and applying them to prevent dismal systems. Economics is called the Dismal Science, for good reason. It's about limits: Satisfying unlimited human wants with limited resources. Economics is the study of allocation of scarce resources. And in any competitive business environment, resources will be limited. I was an Economist before I got into the computer business. We were fond of saying: "There is no such thing as a free lunch", often while we were eating one.

Les Programeurs Miserables

We always hear how rarely computer projects are completed on time and within budget. Should we blame it on technologists? Here's the story of one "late and over budget project."

Scene 1: The office of Manny the Programming Manager in a Fortune 500 firm.

Lily the Lead Programmer enters stage left. Manny looks up expectantly.

Lily: I have the estimate, Manny. It will take approximately 24 months to build that new system.

Manny: *Under his breath, but loud enough for Lily to hear:* Gee, I thought she was a better programmer than that! *To Lily:* Whew, that's two whole years! Dina the Director will never accept that. But wait! I know! What if I got you and your team brand new workstations, and a concierge service to handle some of your daily chores, and sent you all to that productivity seminar in Las Vegas so you can learn the latest programming techniques. Under those conditions, do you think you could do it in, say, 18 months?

L: *Hesitantly* Well, I suppose that might be possible....

M: Good, it's settled then! *Writes down: "18 Months". Does* not *write down workstations, or concierge, or Vegas.* I'll take this to Dina right away. *Exeunt, stage left.*

The Curtain Descends

Narrator: *On the way to Dina's office, through that phenomenon totally unexplained by science but frequently experienced by programming managers, a warp in the Universe causes the ink on the paper to re-arrange its molecules so that "18 Months" now reads "12 Months".*

Scene 2: The office of Dina the Development Director.

Manny the manager enters stage left. Dina looks up expectantly.

Manny: I have the estimate, Dina. It will take approximately 12 months to build that new system.

Dina: *Under her breath, but loud enough for Manny to hear:* Gee, I thought he was a better manager than that! *To Manny:* Whew, that's a whole year! Vince the Vice President will never accept that. But wait! I know! What if I got you a bigger office, and a reserved parking space so you won't waste time trying to park, and sent you to that management seminar in Maui so you can learn the latest motivation techniques. Under those conditions, do you think you could do it in, say, nine months?

M: *Hesitantly* Well, I suppose that might be possible....

D: Good, it's settled then! *Writes down: "9 Months". Does* not *write down office, or parking space, or Maui.* I'll take this to Vince right away. *Gets up, they both exit, stage left.*

The Curtain Descends

This is one play you can safely leave during Intermission. We all know the outcome. A *six*-month project is approved and funded, a deadline set, and sure enough, *24* months later the project is eventually finished. Management decries the undependability of a programming staff that came in *Three Hundred Percent* over budget. They'll blame it on the miserable programmers. But in fact, we actually hit the programmer's original estimate right on the head. As Robert Glass points out in *Software Runaways*, "most cost and schedule targets are set by marketers or customers, next most often by managers, and least often by the technologists who will do the work."

In some cases, management originates the tendency to underestimate. When it's subtly clear a low estimate is expected, not surprisingly you'll get one. And when enough pressure is brought on technical employees to cave and agree to an unreasonable schedule, they'll probably do so.

In other cases, it's self-delusion of management, and to be fair, the programming staff as well, that leads to this problem: "We want it done by a certain date, therefore it must be possible to do it by that date." Or, "I really want to do this project, and if it can't be done within a certain cost it won't be approved, so I'm sure we can do it for that amount." The estimate is inversely proportional to the desire to do the project. This will be especially true if missed deadlines are easily forgiven; the corporate culture becomes "Tell them what they want to hear, the missed deadlines won't matter anyway."

In some cases, the management *uses* this tendency. In *I Sing the Body Electronic*, Fred Moody describes a project at Microsoft where the team agrees to an impossible schedule with an arbitrarily shortened schedule under pressure from Bill Gates himself. Moody concludes: "while giving his employees the means to win he also ensured that they would interpret their victory as defeat. There would be no laurels for them to rest upon; instead they would dive immediately into their next project hoping to redeem themselves." If Moody is right, this strategy might be cold-blooded, it might even be dishonest, but it's hard to argue it's not effective given Microsoft's commercial success.

And many deadlines are set arbitrarily with no actual relation to value, so overrunning the budget is really just missing a meaningless goal, anyway. American President Lines was developing a new computer system to track cargo in the early 1980s. The project got into the usual problems associated with a project in trouble: missed deadlines, cost overruns, and an overall lack of tangible progress. Eventually the manager was fired, and a consultant was interviewed to take over the project. After careful study, the consultant concluded the project was feasible, but that the schedule and budget would need some serious rework. At the meeting where he presented his proposal, the executives were pleased to hear the good news, and asked what modifications he would like. He replied: "Two, Two and Two." What did he mean by that? "Multiply the staff by two and the time by two, and divide the features by two." Naturally, pandemonium broke out, but after everything settled down, the executives ruefully agreed to the scheme. The consultant was as good as his word, and indeed delivered half the originally planned system with twice the staff in twice the time. But the results were extraordinary, the system assured APL a position as the leader in its industry for more than a decade. The original estimate had no relation to the eventual value, which was many times the actual cost even after accounting for the underestimate.

Faster, Cheaper, Better

> **As Economists are wont to emphasize:**
>   We can do it **Faster**…
>   We can do it **Cheaper**…
>   We can do it **Better**…
>   —choose no more than *two* of the above.

Why do you want to put in a new computer system? Let me guess: To make it Faster, Cheaper, and Better. The first rule of economics is, "You can't have it all". Often making something faster will require you to spend more money and or sacrifice some feature that makes it better, cheaper will require slower or less good, and better might slow it down or cost more. You should emphasize one, and choose no more than two, objectives. Be clear upfront and all along which one will be sacrificed if necessary to achieve success. If you have an innovation that supposedly gives all three, beware. Alfred P. Sloan at General Motors once presided over a meeting where a proposal was presented. No one could think of any disadvantages to the proposal. Sloan said if no one can think of anything wrong with the proposal, they'd better not go ahead. He'd never heard of an action with absolutely no downside, so if they hadn't thought of one, they hadn't thought enough. At the next meeting, many reasons were presented why the proposal would have been disastrous, and it was scrapped.

Efficiency is a measure of output versus input, focusing on reducing waste. Most companies don't care as much about the efficiency of an analysis project as they do about its effectiveness, i.e. producing the best system by meeting the business need. Companies are willing to spend hundreds of thousands of dollars on tools and training which will probably not reduce the cost of analysis in any way, if they believe it will give them a better system. Some of the tool vendors claim their analysis techniques will deliver a system at lower cost, but generally because of the efficiency of the programming phase, not the analysis phase.

Sunk Opportunities

The two most important economic principles you need to know about costs are sunk costs and opportunity costs. They frequently occur together, but have also been sighted apart. Sunk costs look to the past: "What's done is done" and opportunity costs look to the future: What could be done.

Sunk Costs are Junked Costs

There is a human reluctance to accept loss. Often in systems development, a project turns out to be too expensive, or takes too long, or just goes off the rails. The sensible thing is to cut your losses and cancel the project. Someone will protest: "We've put umpteen gazillion dollars into this project, we can't throw that away!" But if the project is destined for failure, unless you're buying time to find another job, there is no logic in losing even more money because you don't want to lose face.

> Don't throw good money after bad.

And remember, past consideration is no consideration. "What have you done for me lately?" is the motto. If it's a bad project, pull the plug.

Opportunity Cost

One of the most important concepts from economics is the concept of opportunity cost. Opportunity cost is calculated as the theoretical cost of the profits lost from not taking an alternate course of action, that is the cost of the money you could have made had you pursued another opportunity. For example, if you have a vacant apartment, it is incorrect to say there is no cost in not renting it out. If you rent your apartment to your brother-in-law at below market rate, the extra rent he didn't pay is the opportunity cost of not renting it to someone else. And there is an opportunity cost measured as the difference between the rent your brother-in-law actually pays and what you would get at market rate. In systems, opportunity cost is the other system you could build, or the cost of waiting on a system and its effect on TTM—Time To Market. So don't lose opportunity on unproductive projects.

While you keep sinking, you're losing the opportunity. Retailers learn this early. If you stock and item that doesn't sell, novice retailers have trouble cutting the price below cost and getting them out of the store. What you must do is ruthlessly cut the price, even if you will lose money on those items, in order to free up shelf space for items that will sell. The reluctance to lose the sunk cost in the unpopular item is costing you even more in opportunity cost of the profit you would make on the new item.

The Boehm Curve

It's a postulate of systems analysis is that the cost of changing a program increases exponentially through the SDLC, as illustrated by the Boehm Curve, from Barry W. Boehm's classic, *Software Engineering Economics*, which is still a surprisingly valuable book despite being over two decades old. A design change that would have cost $1 during early analysis might cost hundreds of dollars after the system has been installed.

This used to be unquestioned dogma, and was very much reinforced by my experience: frequently a trivial change in analysis will be all but impossible to fix after implementation. Some developers, however, now question this assumption, arguing modern development methods can reduce the Boehm effect. This debate about shortening development cycles starts with two letters: XP. It stands for eXtreme Programming, and was originally articulated by Kent Beck, but has been endorsed in books on the subject by such luminaries as Martin Fowler, Tom DeMarco, Ward Cunningham, and Erich Gamma (of *Design Patterns* fame). There is a growing series of over a half dozen books and have actually been conferences devoted to this approach. In *Extreme Programming Explained: Embrace Change*, Beck explains the exponential growth could flatten: "If we can flatten the curve, old assumptions about the best way to develop software no longer hold."

XP asserts the Boehm Curve no longer holds, and recommends a development cycle characterized by many iterations of small increments. I personally have no direct experience with the XP approach but have spoken with several developers who tried it with favorable results. They say it works well for the right project. Beck himself points out that this approach is not for every project (something few other methodologists have been honest enough to do). For example, it must be small: five or ten programmers is doable, twenty probably not. Likewise, if you are tied to a complex legacy system the Boehm curve probably does apply and XP probably won't work.

Luddites

In England in the early days of the Industrial Revolution, the workers in the wool and cotton trades became, in the title of Kirkpatrick Sale's book, *Rebels Against the Future*. As work moved from skilled workers at home to unskilled workers in factories, Industrialization ruined their way of life by making it possible for greedy employers to drive wages down and exploit masses of workers for obscene profits. Or so the myth of the Luddites would have us believe. But imagine a *60 Minutes* investigator interviewing one of the downtrodden factory workers:

Mike Wallace: So tell me, how does it feel to work at these wages.

Worker: Great!

Mike: Uh, I thought you'd be angry. You don't mind making less than what wool croppers used to make?

Worker: Hell, no: this is more money than I ever made in my life before.

Mike: But surely you've heard of the Luddites…

Worker: Look, those guys controlled a trade and artificially kept their own wages high at the expense of those of us they considered beneath them. They passed the job from father to son, and were sure to keep the likes of me out of work. Their closed guild would never have allowed me or my children to join. So you see, they aren't just fighting those above them on the economic ladder; they are also keeping us down. And now, thanks to the factories, thousands of us have jobs where only a few of them had jobs before. Serves them right!

Mike (to cameraman): Woops, looks like there's no story here. Let's go over and interview some of those poor, displaced Luddites.

> **Veblen's Principle:**
> **ALL changes help some people and hurt others.**

So technological innovation will probably bring at least some harm to some people, and some of the historically accepted examples of injustice may have had some justice in them. I'm sure most of us have our qualms about where technology is taking us, and whether it's for good or ill. I've thought long and hard and have concluded it is indeed good, and offer three steps in the argument. First, we humans in a technological society live significantly longer than our non-technological counterparts, both past and present. The second observation is that given a choice, the vast majority of people choose the technological lifestyle over the primitive one, and those that reject it find, often to their horror or disgust, that their children embrace it. So although Jacques Ellul argues in *The Technological Bluff* that although we live longer lives, they are not better lives, we must accept that the technological life is better since those with a free choice freely choose it. And third, our lives have less drudgery, more entertainment, and are more interesting than without technology. So the bottom line is: I'm glad I was born into a technologically advanced time and place, and those that disagree might turn off the power to their homes for a week and see if it changes their perspective. You'll face similar quandaries on a smaller scale as a computer systems developer, but I am convinced that on balance, technology improves our lives.

Metcalfe's Law

Metcalfe's Law is stated as: Network value increases with the square of the number of nodes attached to it. It is somewhat uncertain whether Bob Metcalfe, after whom it is named, ever actually said it, and if he did, it was in reference to LANs, not the Internet, but I'm quibbling. Carl Sagan insists that he never said "Billions and Billions" (in his book of the same name); Sherlock Holmes never said "Elementary, my dear Watson"; and Bogart never said, "Play it again, Sam". But they might as well have, and even if they didn't, they probably should have. And Bob Metcalfe could have expressed his law as "Billions and Billions", because that's what his namesake formula computes to.

Yes, this is the same Bob Metcalfe who predicted collapse of the Internet in his column "From the Ether: Predicting the Internet's catastrophic collapse and ghost sites galore in 1996":

"Almost all of the many predictions now being made about 1996 hinge on the Internet's continuing exponential growth. But I predict the Internet, which only just recently got this section here in InfoWorld, will soon go spectacularly supernova and in 1996 catastrophically collapse. Here's why there soon will be only World Wide Web ghost pages."

But I'm quibbling, again, aren't I? Apparently George Gilder actually stated the law, attributing it to Metcalfe, who gamely accepted credit. Not content with the amazing increases implied by the original formulation, in his book *Telecosm*, Gilder restates Metcalfe's Law as *The Law of the Telecosm*: "The value of a network grows by the square of the processing power of all the terminals attached to it." Since processing power increases with Moore's Law, Gilder's Law of the Telecosm would imply you need to factor a doubling every 18 months on top of the squaring. Not to be outdone, Kelly, in *New Rules for the New Economy* argues Metcalfe understates the value of relationships, that the formula is truly exponential, N to the Nth power!

Wait! Stop it! Time for a reality check!

Do the math: Between about 1994 and 1999, the Internet grew about 100 fold, from about a million to 100 million nodes. If Kelly were correct, that would mean the value of the network increased by 100 to the 100th power. That is an extremely large number: it's a googol googols, a one followed by 200 zeroes. A *googol* is 1 followed by a mere 100 zeroes. A googol is a number so large there is nothing to use it on: it's larger than the number of atoms in the universe, and Kelly expects us to accept a googol of googols' increase. In fact, according to Newman, if the entire Universe were filled with protons and electrons, so that no vacant space remained, the total number of protons and electrons would only be 100 to the 55th power. Irrational exuberance indeed, if dollars were the size of atomic particles, you would need a billion, billion, billion, billion, billion, billion, billion, billion, billion (Carl

Sagan would love this, bless his heart!) universes the size of ours to cram in 100 to the 100th dollars! Methinks Mr. Kelly might have overstated just a wee bit.

But even Metcalfe's Law in its original statement, without Kelly's or Gilder's embellishments, cannot hold long mathematically before the Ponzi-scheme effect kicks in. Internet growth has been phenomenal. *When you take a phenomenal increase, and then square it, you get absurdity.* It's probably slowed of late, but for several years the Internet was doubling in size every nine months, a compound rate of about 150 percent per annum. Metcalfe's Law implies value increased at a compound rate of 535 percent per annum! Set yourself up a spreadsheet and see the result of that kind of growth. Let's begin at the beginning. In 1971, ARPANet, the Internet precursor, linked 23 sites. ARPA spent thousands creating this humble beginning, but let's just say each connection was worth only what an AOL or MSN connection would cost today, about $23 per month. That means today the average node is worth over $300 million a month, and the Internet is worth $90 *thousand trillion* per month in total! There ain't that much money in the World: it's about 80,000 US economies! Okay, so maybe the squaring didn't start at the beginning. At the 150% rate we've been growing, were increasing 10 fold about every three to four years, but squaring gives us a 100-fold increase in value in that same period. Those crybaby customers who objected to the $2 per month increase at AOL are wrenching, grasping, ungrateful cheapskates, since the value of each connection must have increased by well over $2 *hundred* per month—why were they complaining about a lousy two bucks?!?

So the math doesn't work, but how about the theory? It is possible to question a key underlying assumption, to wit: that the Law of Diminishing Returns—which states that as a factor increases, there will be a decrease in the marginal benefit from a given increase that factor of production—doesn't apply to a network. As Shapiro & Varian say in *Information Rules*: "Technology changes, economic laws do not." Consider an individual Net user, such as myself. If Internet growth is proceeding at anything like its historic rate, several hundred new users are joining the wired world every second, even as I sleep! Is the value of my node increasing geometrically as a result? I will never have any contact with the vast majority of these individuals. And truth to be told, I don't *want* to have any contact with most of them. So, no, they aren't increasing the value of the Internet to me at all. Not everyone has something worth listening to. In *Emergence: the Connected lives of Ants, Brains, Cities and Software*, Johnson considers the often familiar of the Internet as a huge brain and concludes its ratio of growth to order is characteristic of not a brain, but a brain *tumor*.

How about business on the Internet? Surely the e-commerce community will derive value from these newbies. Perhaps, but certainly not at a geometrically increasing rate; in fact, the rate is *diminishing* at the margin. How's that? The value of new entrants to the world of e-business is clearly only the discounted value of the eventual profits derived from them. The average entrant has a lower income than the average person already on line, so the potential marginal contribution to e-commerce is declining, not increasing at all, much less increasing geometrically. We've long passed Pareto optimality with the 20% of customers representing 80% of the income. In fact, considerably more of the world's disposable income is already on-line than still off-line. So if Metcalfe's Law ever did hold, it doesn't anymore. You wouldn't expect it to, rather than continuing steeply upward we expect to see an S-shaped curve with growth leveling off.

Originally Metcalfe was clearly talking about networks and computer nodes, but it's gone beyond that. *The X-Economy*: "The value of a network is equal to the square of its members—whether computers, phones or value chain participants." Shapiro &Varian in *Information Rules* apply the concept of network externalities, which they discuss with Metcalfe's Law, to fax machines, and even buyers of a given product, such as Mac Users as a network. The authors' don't actually say Metcalfe's Law would apply, but this again argues against taking the Law literally: these kinds of networks always existed, so that would suggest the Law has been operating for centuries, and would also operate on the off-line competitors to the Internet, thus removing any special advantage. Wouldn't spiders be the riches creatures on earth?

Note the phenomenal increases in Internet users can't continue much longer in any event: We're less than two doublings away from everyone with a telephone. A further four to five doublings will require us to go to literally universal access, because it will exceed the population of Earth, so we'll have to boldly go out into the Universe to find more users. Of course if we talk nodes or computers instead of people, the doubling could continue indefinitely. It's said there are already several times as many computers (microprocessors) as people on Earth, but they are not as valuable as people since they don't have their own credit cards (yet).

But I always interpreted Metcalfe's Law metaphorically rather than as an actual statement of mathematical certitude. In Mr. Metcalfe's defense, it appears he made a casual remark that Gilder hyperbolically stated as a law; the Law was never mathematically demonstrated, and wasn't intended to be. Nonetheless, Metcalfe's Law should not be simply dismissed. Murphy's Law, "Anything that can go wrong, will go wrong" is a Law, a useful Law, and yes, even a true Law. It is irrefutably empirically demonstrable that the vast majority of things that can go wrong, do NOT go wrong, but Murphy's Law is a truth that needs no proof to anyone who has ever worked on a complex system.

In *The Lexus and the Olive Tree*, Friedman refers to Moore's Law, not Metcalfe's, but describes the difference between the old Cold War paradigm and globalization in network terms: "In the Cold War, the most frequently asked question was: 'Who's side are you on?' In globalization, the most frequently asked question is: 'To what extent are you connected to everyone?' In the Cold War, the second most frequently asked question was: 'How big is your missile?' In globalization, the second most frequently asked question is: 'How fast is your modem?' "Both Friedman and Metcalfe are right: the network might not be the computer, but the computer that is not on the network may become irrelevant. And the business. And even the person.

Learning Curve

One of my pet peeves is the popular misunderstanding of the Learning Curve. Like *The Ugly American*, people always get it backwards. The "Ugly American" in the book was a kind, caring individual, as opposed to the Handsome American, who was obnoxious. Whenever you hear someone describe an American behaving boorishly abroad as an ugly American, you can be sure they haven't read the book: It was the handsome American who was the lout. The Learning Curve is likewise the opposite of what most people think.

A Learning Curve shows a decline in unit cost as we gain experience. Note the original learning curve, from Economics: It slopes down to the right, so you don't "climb the learning curve", you slide down it. And a "steep learning curve" means it's *easy* to learn. In everyday speech, these characteristics are often reversed, "a steep learning curve" intended to mean hard to learn.

The Pareto Principle

The Pareto Principle, also known as the 80/20 Rule, is named after Vilfredo Pareto, an Italian economist, who noted that in distributions 80 percent of the dividend usually goes to 20 percent of the observations. For example, 80 percent of the wealth is held by the richest 20 percent of households, 80 percent of the workers are employed by the largest 20 percent of companies, etc. By this reckoning, 80 percent of your problems will be caused by 20 percent of your bugs, or cases, or whatever.

In many circumstances the 80/20 rule becomes the 90/10 rule: 90 percent of the problems are caused by 10 percent of the items. So the opportunity is to be sure to find all of the 10 to 20 percent of items that will cause most of the problems, and then reduce the other problems as much as you can. Include the critical items you can't operate without, look inside complicated processes in which the chance of error is high, and consider the past history of problems you've encountered from each system.

Self-Fulfilling Prophecies

Self-fulfilling Prophecies are an interesting phenomenon. They happen when people believe something is going to happen, and then because of these beliefs, unintentionally cause the event to actually happen. For example, if people believe a bank is going to fail, they rush to withdraw their money from the bank. If enough people do this, the bank will fail, even if its finances are sound. The stock market has a tendency to go where everyone thinks it will: if most investors think prices will rise, they probably will, because buyers will be willing to pay more and sellers will expect more.

The same can be true of your systems development effort. In many cases, whether you think you can, or you think you can't, you're right. If the team becomes convinced they are going to fail, they'll stop putting in serious effort, their morale and effort will flag, and sure enough, they'll fail.

> Whether you believe you can, or
> Believe you can't
> You are right.

I once worked on a project where we were all inexperienced. None of us new what we were doing, so we committed to what we now all know was an impossible task. Fortunately, we were so dumb we didn't know enough to know the task was impossible, so we just did it! Only after we'd done it did we realize it was impossible.

Changes in Closet

Okay, you've been working hard on this stuff, so now I'm going to tell you to take a break, this time to see a movie. Every Systems Analyst must see *Mr. Blandings Builds His Dream House*, based on the book by Eric Hodgins, with Cary Grant as Jim Blandings, and Myrna Loy as Muriel Blandings. Although it was made in 1948, and is about building a house, not a system per se, it's probably the best movie on projects and systems ever made. I like to play the "Changes in Closet" sequence to my class at UC Berkeley Extension.

The notation "Changes in Closet" is written on an outrageously large bill for modifications supposedly authorized by Mrs. Blandings. It turns out there were four pieces of flagstone left over from the porch that were going to be thrown away. Mrs. Blandings asked the contractor to put them on the floor of the pantry closet she called her "flower room". She said she wanted it to be nice and dry. "Well, you're the doctor" he said. The contractor interpreted "nice and dry" to require a drain. This needed a carpenter to rip out the floor, which went under the wall so they knocked that out, too. Then they needed to chop off a joist to make room for a cradle, weakening said joist, and requiring iron straps for a large pan to hold the cement. Because of the added weight, they needed a lolly column to support the floor. The pan would sit on the hot and cold water pipes and the 220-volt electrical cable. So they needed a plumber to re-angle the drainpipes under the entire house and move the hot and cold water pipes, and an electrician had to reroute the 220-volt electrical cabling. Then a carpenter and a plasterer put the wall and floor back. Cost for the four old stones that were to be thrown away added something like a fifth of what the entire house, including 35 acres of land, had cost!

The lessons? A seemingly simple change can be very costly; and something that would have been trivial at the beginning is extremely expensive after a lot of work has been done. Don't forget technicians will assume you know what's involved when you ask for something, so beware.

6

THE KARMA OF CULTURE

All truth lies buried in paradox.
—George Bernard Shaw

The Right Endeavor is along the path of people and cultural enlightenment. So this chapter speaks of people, and includes cultural impacts of systems. Culture is affected by Karma. Karma is the concept that actions set off reactions that affect future events. This is very true in analysis, where slight misperceptions can ripple back as a tsunami. The best illustration of Karma I've ever seen was a filmstrip I saw in Driver Ed in High School. The filmmakers had no idea they were illustrating Karma when they showed an example of an impatient man on his way to work discourteously cutting off another driver. The man went on his way, but the driver who was cut off seethed, and went on to cut another driver off in his anger. That driver then went on to cut another motorist off, who cut another off, and so on. The cycle continued throughout the workday as the first driver obliviously worked away. At the end of the day the man left work and was crashed into by, you guessed it, the latest angry driver caused by his transgression of that morning. The film ended with the man protesting: "Why do these bad things always happen to me, the good driver!"

Whether or not you accept Karma as a cosmic force, there is no question actions reverberate in systems development. Lack of care in the early stages of the life cycle to clarify goals and requirements will come back to haunt you in the next life, namely the next phase of the project. As the Beatles said: "In the end, the love you take is equal to the love you make".

This chapter of the book will concentrate on the interpersonal aspects of analysis. Drawn from my UC Berkeley Extension class, *The Systems Analyst as Internal Consultant*, this portion focuses on the people and cultural problems you'll encounter doing analysis. I almost called this chapter The People Path, because it talks a lot about people problems, as a group and in groups. We'll look at rules, aphorisms and guidelines for discovery and harmony to help you start and finish your present analysis assignment with enough good Karma left over to get you through the next one. Incidentally, my book based on the course, *The Systems Analyst as Internal Consultant*, has more material on this topic.

A Problem Like Any Other

The good news is that the worst problems associated with analysis are not technical—they're people problems. The bad news is that *all* the problems turn out to be people problems once you analyze them. Perhaps expectations were too high, requirements or capabilities were misunderstood, or someone didn't make the connection. And despite the fact that systems analysts are first and foremost problem solvers, we tend to lose all our problem-solving skills when confronted with a people problem. With any other problem, we'll go through the proven cycle: *analyze* the problem; *design* a solution; *test* it, and if it works; *implement* it. And then *maintain* it. But it never occurs to us that exactly these same steps can be used with people problems. So if you have a problem employee, coworker or user, try to solve it like you would any other problem, using the problem-solving skills you've developed as an analyst

Sometimes using a little Judo psychology on a difficult person can turn the situation around. Jūdō is literally "the gentle way", and suggests you should try to turn anger away, not with force, but by rolling with the attack. And if Judo doesn't work, there is always Karate.

The Two Cultures

C.P. Snow delivered his lecture on *The Two Cultures* in 1959. He suggested that intellectual life divided into two isolated cultures, with Science on one side, versus the Arts and Humanities—'the literary Intellectuals'—on the other. We are likewise faced with two cultures in developing a computer system. Guy Kawasaki in *The Macintosh Way* calls them "T-Shirts" and "Ties" for their sartorial preferences: T-Shirts are commonly worn by Technologists such as programmers; Ties are de rigueur in the business departments in typical companies and marketing departments in high-tech firms. Various terms are used to describe the business side, the people we systems analysts build computer systems for: business, client, subject matter experts. *User* is probably the most common term, but it has bad connotations: "Users are losers," according to the US Government, although referring to drug users. So we often call them the "business" in this book.

As a systems analyst, a critical part of your job is to provide a bridge between these two cultures; you must be bicultural to bring the two disciplines together. My consulting firm's slogan is *"Zen & Analysis: Business Art and Systems Science"*. In this day of the indispensable computer, you must be able to think from both a business and a technical perspective if you are to design effective business solutions.

Is analysis more an art, or a science? At this stage of history, I could *not* have named this book *Zen and the Science of Systems Analysis*, Robert Pirsig aside. In fact, even programming has a lot of Art to it. Donald Knuth, the Stanford professor emeritus, recipient of numerous awards and honors, including the ACM Turing Award, and the President's Medal of Science, named his monumental opus, called "the definitive description of classical computer science", you guessed it: *The ART of Computer Programming*. I once attended a talk at Cisco Systems in Silicon Valley. The lecturer gave a "here's how it's done at Cisco" perspective. He entitled his talk "Requirements Analysis: the Art and the Science". His first slide was Webster's definitions of Art and of Science. He then said: "Of course, Systems development is more an Art than a Science. I'll go over the Science quickly first, because that's the easy part".

If your experience and background make you lean to one side, try to become a little of the other. Systems development requires both programming and analysis. Moving from a programmer to an analyst, or from business to IT, involves becoming and artful scientist or a scientific artist. Developing a system is not a science! The system's success lies not with scientific algorithms, but the artsy heuristics.

Feasibility Studies

What's the best way to gain deep insight into the culture of any IT organization? Ask about how (or if) they conduct feasibility studies. The feasibility study is the first step in developing a system, and indeed the first phase of many SDLCs. It may be called something else, perhaps the concept or planning phase, but what I mean by feasibility study is the method, formal or informal, by which projects are selected for approval and funding—so call it project approval if you prefer. Whatever else the deliverable of a feasibility study is, its primary product is funding for the project. A feasibility study can be a months-long inquiry into new technology including the meaning of life and the nature of time and space, and produce a tome spanning several volumes; or it might consist of the CEO tossing you an article from an in-flight magazine and saying "Do it!" (In fact, the wise CIO has a team of people who sole job it is to surreptitiously sweep any aircraft the CEO will be boarding and remove all in-flight magazines.) In some organizations the feasibility study is actually conducted as part of an ISP, a formal Information Systems Plan of ponderous proportions.

The attitude toward feasibility studies can give great insight to the culture of an organization. When I worked for the State of California, we were required to do a feasibility study for any project over a certain amount; I think it was $25,000. We were planning a new system that would involve on-line access from dozens of State offices to a huge database. Needless to say, this project would exceed the $25,000 threshold so we had to do a feasibility study. But wait, the feasibility study required considerable research, and a cost benefit analysis with return on investment (ROI) calculated over the life of the project. You guessed it, the feasibility study itself would cost more than $25,000, so we needed to do a feasibility study for the feasibility study. And guess what? *That* feasibility study would exceed the threshold. And on and on. So the culture at the State was to study things.

After the State, I went to work for American President Lines (APL). At the time, it was a very nimble and fast growing company. One of my early assignments was to check out an old computer system that was being used in the ship terminal. I looked it over, and reported to my boss we should just scrap the old system and buy new computers at a cost of some hundreds of thousands of dollars. "Okay, go buy them", she said without hesitation. I was taken aback, assuming I would have had to spend weeks on feasibility studies. "Well, umm, won't someone have to sign for them?" I stammered. "Oh, don't you have a pen? Here, borrow mine." And that was it.

Culture can change over time, and that is often first reflected in the feasibility study. American President Lines has changed since my days there, in fact the official name is now "APL", not American President Lines, as the firm isn't American, having been acquired by a Singapore firm. It became less entrepreneurial, and not nearly as fast as before: they began to study things more.

A Hot New Video

This is a story about a project conducted by the Highway Transportation Division of an anonymous banana-shaped State on the West Coast of the United States that has a city we'll call "San Francisco" in it. It seems they were interested in determining the commute patterns in this mythical San Francisco area so as to design the best freeways. And so they set up some video cameras at some strategic points and taped the cars driving past. A small army of data entry clerks watched the videos, typed the license plate numbers in, and a survey was mailed to the registered owner of each vehicle asking where they were coming from and going to. Quite a feat of information processing.

The survey's major conclusion: At any given time, a great many people are *not supposed to be where they are!* Spouses who were supposed to be at home and workers in company cars who were supposed to be home sick called, desperately seeking help because their sins were discovered when the wrong person opened the survey. The authorities hastily sent out a vaguely enough worded letter to the affect of: "You might have received a survey in error" (although of course there was no error) to let the wanderers off the hook.

> So the lesson:
> Think about the impact of your actions.

Teamwork

In the Programming classes I teach at the College of Alameda, I give the students the option of completing the all-important project as a team. The project is heavily weighted such that it pretty much determines the grade for the course. The rule is: the team receives a single grade; and each team member gets the same grade. For example, ten points are awarded for presenting the project to the class. All members receive the ten points, even if those that don't participate in the demo, in fact they get the ten points even if they are absent on the day of the presentation. This is because the major learning goal from the exercise is teamwork, and I learned something about teamwork in the Army.

Whatever else you want to say about it, there is probably no more successful team building organization than the Army. The Army consistently takes a group of unrelated individuals from different backgrounds and molds a group of soldiers literally willing to die for one another. In a RAND Corporation study conducted for the US Army entitled *The "Virtual Corporation" and Army Organization*, Fukuyama & Shulsky discuss organizational trends in the commercial sector. Surprisingly, despite the stereotype of an army as the ultimate in C&C (Command & Control), many of the commercial-sector initiatives of the Nineties first appeared in the military, shown by examples from Napoleon, to Blitzkrieg, to the US Army.

One policy I observed in the Army is to always treat the team as a team. The team will be rewarded and punished together, as a team. If everyone does well, everyone does well; if anyone fails, everyone fails. Remember that an army travels at the speed of the slowest marcher, and so with teams. So if teambuilding is your goal, recognition and rewards should be given to the group, not to individuals. Takeuchi & Nonaka say Japanese companies establish evaluation and reward systems based on group performance. They are a subtle way to exercise control over new product development teams. For example, Canon (named, incidentally, after the Buddhist goddess of Mercy, not for artillery) applies for patents in the name of a group.

A team is not a team unless the team is greater than the sum of its members. One time I had two young men in the class who were your typical nerds. They were doing a very impressive project; I saw them in the lab at all hours, and most of the questions they asked me were beyond even my experience, as they were getting into some pretty advanced stuff. So I was quite pleased when I received their project package: excellent technically, and professionally presented.

Only one surprise. There were *three* names on the cover. Strange. I hadn't seen this third person working in the lab with them at all. So I asked them about it, and the two nerds earnestly insisted the third team member was absolutely vital to the success of this project; in fact I could flunk them if I wanted but their teammate absolutely deserved an A+. Pretty strange, huh?

Oh, one small detail I neglected to mention. The third team member was a strikingly attractive young woman.

So what to do? In the end, I decided to follow the stated rule, and give all the team members, including the young woman, the A+ the project deserved. There were several reasons for this, one being that I feel I must respect my students, even to the extent of believing what they say even when there is strong evidence to the contrary. But from a managerial perspective, the young lady *did* contribute significantly to the success of the project, in that it certainly would not have been as impressive had she not been on the team. A lot of the nerds' motivation was to get *her* an A+. These two guys would gladly have jumped off the Golden Gate Bridge for her, so working extra hard on a class project was easy enough for them.

I've seen other team dynamics at work, although not as blatant. Sometimes a person who is only an average performer contributes to team morale in such a way as to enhance the entire effort. Take care when you disturb a well functioning team; even the least performer by objective criteria might be essential to the success. Team spirit is a fragile commodity and you best not tamper with it unnecessarily.

Perceptions Are Reality

Sometimes you can effectively enforce rules without enforcing them at all. Another War story: When I was drafted into the army, a large number of us were taken to a large room and lined up with our bags and suitcases and told to dump out our bags into small squares painted on the floor about three feet square. Several MPs (Military Police) with dogs were standing by, and there were several 55-gallon barrels located around the room.

The officer in charge came to the microphone and said, "We're about to conduct a search of your belongings. If we find any contraband, you can be sure you'll be severely punished. But before we conduct the search, we will leave the room for five minutes. He pointed to the barrels. While we're out, you can drop anything you'd like into the barrels. You will not be punished for any contraband you drop in there, but if, on our return, we find any drugs, alcohol or weapons, you'll be doing hard labor at Fort Leavenworth before you know what happened to you."

The officer, MP's and dogs then left the room. As the minutes passed, one by one some of my fellow inductees went to the barrels and dropped something in. All the barrels were overflowing with drugs, booze, guns, knives, and brass knuckles by the time the officer returned, without the escort. He went to the microphone and announced: "Thank you, you can pack up your bags and leave now" and we were allowed to leave without any search.

So the strategy was that once you make everyone believe they can't get away with something, it isn't necessary to actually implement a plan to stop them. Sometimes security on computers works this way. Like a "Speed Limit Enforced by Radar" sign in town with no radar, if everyone thinks the computer is secure, it is. If you can't afford a surveillance camera, put up a fake camera: Make them think they're being watched.

Empathy with Users

After graduating from Cal State Sacramento (CSUS) with a degree in Economics, I went to work as an economist for the State of California, in which capacity I was a user of computer systems. I got into programming after I was told that the computer work for my survey, which would require about three weeks effort, would probably reach the top of the queue in about two years! I figured: "Maybe I could get the three weeks' work done in less than two years by doing it myself", and managed to do so. As the other economists took advantage of my growing skill I gradually found myself programming full time. I was a good enough economist to see programmers were more in demand than economists so I changed careers and became a programmer. Now that I'm on the other side, whenever I'm dealing with clients I try to remember my own experiences as a poor little frustrated user, just trying to get a little help from the computer department. This empathy with my users and clients often helps me understand the situation better than others who do not have the benefit of the user's perspective.

Years later, after I'd been in systems for a while, I was teaching a group of users how to use computers and was absolutely astounded at how stupid they were. Dumb as dirt! They did not even know the most basic concepts about computers. Amazing, since some of them were college graduates, and held well paying positions. That weekend I happened to be cleaning out a closet and came across a booklet I'd received way back when I was a junior economist from a class called something like "Computers for Nontechnical People". As I flipped through the book and noticed the notes I had made a few years before, I realized I had been even dumber than those users I was teaching. After years of working with technology you forget that you weren't born knowing this stuff.

Some years after desktop computers became commonplace on users' desks, the company I was working for began giving PCs to the programming staff (IT is always the last to automate). I came back to my desk to find a new PC there. I turned it on, but it didn't seem to work, so I figured it hadn't been connected yet. I called the helpdesk, and after trying some things, one of the technicians came down. To make a long story short, I had turned on the CPU, but not the monitor. I only saw one of the switches, and I didn't realize the CPU and monitor were separate pieces. The monitor was sitting on top of the CPU, and I thought it was permanently attached. In fact, when I tried to move it to a better location, I almost dropped the monitor when it slid off the CPU. In my defense, I have to argue that that design is not that obvious. The Macintosh and iMac, for example, are designed with integrated CPU and monitor, so it *could* have been designed that way.

As with many technological things, it's intuitively obvious, once you've seen it. Someone trying to set up their first home computer faces a daunting task. Once you know how the plugs are designed, it's obvious where they go, but the first time you try to plug in one of those plugs can be gut wrenching. You can see all those little pins, which are obviously fragile. How hard should you push? After you've done it a few times, you know immediately when you're pushing too hard, so you have it in the wrong slot or have it upside down. But the first time you have no idea. So remember how helpless you felt at first and temper your arrogance with empathy.

Apple Corps

The Macintosh Group at Apple Computer was special. And special people get special treatment. Steve Jobs had assumed personal command over this group and separated them from the rest of Apple Computer. They had their own special building, with a pirate flag flying over it. And the Mac people were very pleased. When they traveled, unlike the rest of the company, they traveled *first class*. First class people travel first class. And the Mac people were very pleased. And their soft drinks were free, provided by the company, and the Mac people were very pleased. And they knew they were better than anyone, because their leader, Steve Jobs, told them so. So the Macintosh people were very pleased with themselves, and very happy with Apple Computer.

One day it was decided to integrate the Macintosh Group back into the company. And since the Mac people were special, Steve decreed no Mac person would report to any non-Mac person after the merger. If two groups merged, the Mac Group leader would become the leader of the combined group. If a Mac person was alone in a group, he'd be the group leader. Many of them were elevated to managerial and supervisory roles because of this rule. And the Mac people were very pleased.

Until they began to look through the personnel folders of their new charges. It became obvious the salary scales in the Mac group had been significantly lower than the rest of the company. The new leader of a group of non-Mac people discovered he was the lowest paid person in the group! All of his subordinates made more than he did.

And the Mac people were _not_ very pleased. Some formerly loyal and enthusiastic workers actually left the company. So the lesson is that, logically or not, people usually measure satisfaction based on their relative standing, not their absolute standing. Often someone who is very pleased with the current situation will become very dissatisfied upon discovering someone else in a similar situation is getting a better deal. Keep this in mind when planning new systems and the reward structures associated with them.

> **People Judge their Situation not Absolutely,**
> **But Relative to Other People**

In most American companies it is considered bad form to discuss salaries. In some companies, it's even a disciplinary offense. HR Departments want rigid security to protect salary information. In several database courses I've taken, the example used to explain database views, that restrict access to certain fields, was the obvious need to have a view of personnel information that excluded salary to avoid enquiring minds. Salaries are kept secret to preserve "employee's privacy". Yeah, and so there won't be grumbling about inequitable treatment.

I've worked in private industry where there was a secret-salary policy. But I've also worked for a State government, where the salary for each position was established by law, and so a matter public record. Morale did not collapse based on the knowledge of one another's salary. In fact, it had clear benefits. You knew you wanted to work for that next promotion because you knew exactly how much more you'd make when promoted.

And there was probably less dissension, given that people were not disgruntled in the mistaken belief they were underpaid. When I was at American President Lines, an employee survey revealed *every* identifiable group of employees in the company thought they were underpaid relative to other groups! That's mathematically impossible! So at an absolute minimum, 50% of the employees incorrectly felt they were being treated unfairly, which would have been impossible if they knew the true salaries.

It seems to me that if you are running a fair and equitable compensation system you should have no problem with revealing salaries.

The JAD Session from Hell

Many of you probably have experienced, and those of you that haven't surely will, the user Forest/Tree problem. Imagine an analyst conducting a JAD (Joint Application Development) session, when the following exchange occurs:

Analyst: "Let's assume we're selling widgets"

User: "What are widgets?"

"Just some arbitrary product."

"We don't sell any arbitrated products."

"Okay, what do you sell?"

The user begins a long litany of items describing the product line in numbing detail. The analyst picks one out, and manages to stop him. "Okay let's say we're selling frabistats." So here we'll put the quantity, say 2 or 3.

"We only sell frabistats by the pair!"

Someone else: "No, the size 8 frabistats can be sold individually."

You: "Okay a pair frabistats, say they cost $5."

"Don't be crazy, frabistats are more like $50."

"Okay, $50."

"But none of our frabistats are $50. Some are $45, some $55, but none are $50."

"Okay, $45 then."

"No, the $45 frabistats are on sale for $39.99 this week."

"Okay, to simplify the math in our example, let's say $40."

But they're not $40, they're 39.99!

    Etc.

    Etc.

    Etc.

The users in this case were being very precise, which was actually causing a problem, and interfering with analysis. Take our familiar kotowaza, "Sen Ri no Michi mo Ippo kara", which you recall means "Even a Journey of a Thousand Miles starts from One Step". To be precise, the distance referred to was in Ri, the Olde Japanese measure of distance, about 2½ miles. So precision would require that we translate the kotowaza "Even a Journey of 2,443.1398 Miles starts from One Step". Or perhaps "Even a Journey of a Thousand Miles starts from

0.409332787556283 Step". But that would obviously ruin the poetry. This is the kind of judgment translators, as well as analysts, must face, and the Zen they need to strike the balance between precision and clarity. For an in-depth discussion of the questions faced in translating one language to another, read Douglas Hofstadter's *Le Ton beau de Marot*. It uses an Olde French poem to explore the problems of translation. The various renditions can become a bit tedious, so you might want to scan over them, but anyone interested in representations of languages, including systems analysts, should read this book. Hofstadter was one of the first Computer Scientists in the World, so his work relates directly to computing.

> **Don't Let**
> **Precision Prevent Clarity**

Or consider another example, this time trying to state a rule, from Marvin Minsky's *The Society of Mind*. We all know birds fly. But to be more precise: "Birds can fly, unless they are penguins and ostriches, or if they happen to be dead, or have broken wings, or are confined to cages, or have their feet stuck in cement, or have undergone experiences so dreadful as to render them psychologically incapable of flight." This is another case where we walk a line between two sides of Yin and Yang, where Zen Analysis skills can help us make the right decision.

Of Hottentots and Analysts

There's an old anthropological canard to the effect that the Hottentots of Africa only have three numbers in their language: 1, 2, and "more than two", or "many". On investigation, they are in fact able to communicate large numbers by repeating and stressing their word for many. It turns out that Hottentots actually have a better number sense than Westerners, or at least Oxford undergraduates, since when shown a certain picture of a group of antelopes all Hottentots agree there are "*many*, many", not "many, many" or "many, *many*". Show the same picture to a group of English college students and the estimates range from "a dozen" to "several hundred".

So the Hottentots were the victim of a misunderstanding, but extensive anthropological field research has led to the astounding conclusion: Even if they had only the three numbers, the Hottentots would be more advanced than computer programmers. It seems programmers have only *two* numbers: one and many. That's because to a programmer, a routine will either execute once, or it will execute more than once. If more than once, it needs a control structure or loop around it, if once, it doesn't. To a programmer, once the loop is in place, the routine can execute once, or execute a million times—it makes no difference to the programmer. And of course the range of estimates you'll receive from programmers for a given task can be phenomenal, so they clearly can't estimate as well as the Hottentots, or even the Oxonians.

Analysts, on the other hand, are a bit more advanced than programmers, although they only come up to the level of the mythical Hottentots. They have three numbers, assuming you will accept that zero is a number. For example, for an ERD relationship they need to know, like the programmer, whether there are one or many. But then they need to figure out if it could be zero, that is, if the relationship is mandatory. So analysts count: zero, one, many.

International Bus Tour

I know someone who escorts bus tours through Europe, accompanying a group for two or three weeks, handling the logistics, and lecturing on the sights along the way. Every trip it takes some diplomacy to handle the problem of who gets to sit in which seat. Of course there are exceptions, but she noticed this pattern in the opinions as to how the seats should be allocated.

Americans feel that seats are reserved for the duration of the trip. If you get up early the first day, you can claim the best seat, and it should be yours for the entire trip. Like a land claim in the Old West, once you've staked your claim you have squatter's rights.

Europeans think each day is a new day: Each day the seats are up for grabs, first come first served. You claim a seat for the entire day, but not the entire trip.

Asians believe in sharing. Whoever had the best seat yesterday should certainly not get it today, and certainly no person should suffer in the worst seat two days in a row. Over the course of the trip everyone should have had the best and the worst seats at various times.

Check your cultural assumptions. There are obviously advantages and disadvantages to each way, and each is fair by some reckonings. Make sure your solutions consider national, local and even corporate cultures. Here are a few stories that illustrate how cultural perspective can vary:

Why did it Rain?

When I was living in Japan a group of my friends and I had planned for several weeks to have a picnic in Meiji Park in Tokyo. When the day came for the picnic it was pouring down rain. When my Japanese friend told me the picnic was cancelled, I looked at him and said: "Oh, why did it have to rain today!?!"

My friend scratched his head, then began looking up words in his dictionary. I was surprised by this because his English was quite good. Finally, he had the words he needed: "There's a high pressure cell over Korea that's drawing moist air up from the south, meeting cold air from the north, causing the precipitation over Japan."

Since he was always interested in learning about the English language and American culture, I explained to him that "why did it have to rain today" was a rhetorical question, and in fact, its true meaning was "I really feel bad we can't have our picnic today!"

This astounded my friend. He opened a guidebook written for Americans in Japan and quoted: "Japanese are inscrutable, and make an art of hiding their emotions. They often find it difficult to express their true feelings." He then asked me: "How can this be, since as a Japanese, I have no trouble at all saying "I really feel bad we can't have our picnic today!", and yet you find it hard to say so directly. I could only offer sheepishly: "I guess Americans tend to be inscrutable, and make an art of hiding their emotions. They often find it difficult to express their true feelings."

No Problem?

The meaning of a word can change based on its cultural context. I was on call for the Accounts Payable System one night when I got a call from the Helpdesk telling me there was some problem in Japan. When I was connected to the Tokyo office I asked about the problem.

"Oh, no, Patrick-san, we have *no problem* with the Accounts Payable System." he told me.

"The helpdesk seems to think you have a problem."

"Oh, no, we have *no problem* with the Accounts Payable System. It is a very good system. We like it very much."

I was tempted to go back to sleep, but on a hunch I probed further: "Tell me, how many invoices have you processed today?"

"Well, uh, we have been able to process no invoices today."

"And how many payments have you made?"

"We have been able to make no payments today."

"Takesako-san, if you have been unable to process invoices and make payments, I assure you: *You have a <u>problem</u> with the Accounts Payable System!*"

Be aware of culture and its influence, both national culture and corporate culture. In this case, the polite Japanese manager did not wish to criticize the system to someone he knew had worked on developing it, for fear I might lose face. If I had asked about a "situation" instead of a problem, things would have gone smoother.

Writing it Down

I trained a group of users in Seoul, Korea how to use the same Accounts Payable System when it was first installed. The students were very attentive, and carefully took notes. When I told them how to enter a payable, they all carefully wrote it down. Then I told them how to make a payment, and they all carefully wrote it down. And I told them how to cancel an invoice, and they all carefully wrote it down.

And then I told them a little joke. And they all carefully wrote it down.

So I said: "No, don't write that down!"

And they all carefully wrote *that* down.

The realization struck: "They don't understand a single word I'm saying!" So it was time to try something else. I set aside the training material that had been carefully prepared, at great expense, by my boss. This was a serious decision, since my boss had invested a great deal of time in the material, and was very proud of it. She was of course asleep in the US at the time and so it was not logical to contact her.

Instead of using the training material, for the next four days we had the students bring examples of their work and demonstrated how to do each task. Things seemed to go well enough, and I returned to the US without further incident, or reference to the training material.

When I returned, my boss asked me about the trip. Obviously fishing for a compliment, she honed in on the training material. And so I had a tremendous battle with my conscience: do I lie, or tell her the truth. After a tremendous struggle, my conscience won: I decided to lie. "Your training material was invaluable."

And so that incident was over, or so I thought. About six months later, however, the company decided to do an audit of the new system. Managers would travel to each country where the system was now being used, and assess how well the training and installation had gone. I thought all hope was lost when it turned out my boss would be auditing Korea. So I spent a little time updating my résumé just in case I couldn't make her see the humor, or at least the logic, of the situation when she returned.

Sure enough, when I came into the office the day of her return, I had a message from my boss: "Come see me right away, I need to talk to you about the training in Seoul."

To make a long story short, she wanted to see me because on every measure, Korea had scored the *best* of all the sites! They were processing more invoices with fewer errors than any other site, by a significant margin. So I told her: "Wow, and I never could have done it without your training material!"

A Puzzling Contradiction

Research leads to a puzzling contradiction. None of the books or articles you'll read suggest humiliating employees as a management style. Yet several important projects were led this way. Consider Steve Jobs: Steven Levy tells us in *Insanely Great* that Steve often humiliated his subordinates, even when he himself was unqualified to judge the work.

Or consider Bill Gates, whose favorite phrase is said to be "That's the Stupidest Thing I ever Heard": Fred Moody recounts in *I Sing the Body Electronic* how Bill Gates might explode into a tantrum at a meeting. The expectation that the workplace will be a safe and pleasant environment, not a fearful place, is misplaced. As former Intel CEO Andy Grove said in *Only the Paranoid Survive*:

"The quality guru W. Edwards Deming advocated stamping out fear in corporations. I have trouble with the simple-mindedness of this dictum. The most important role of managers is to create an environment in which people are passionately dedicated to winning in the marketplace. Fear plays an important role in creating and maintaining such passion."

Mike Wilson called his book *The Difference Between God and Larry Ellison*: *God Doesn't Think He's Larry Ellison*.

So the puzzlement is this: it seems that despite what we might think about management styles, it appears there is no correlation between humanity and success in projects!

The Dangerous One

Babe Ruth was the home-run king. He held the Major League record for home runs until Hank Aaron passed him. But many people don't realize he was also the strikeout king. He held the Major League record for strikeouts—until Hank Aaron passed him. The point is you will never achieve greatness if you won't take a chance. This same point is made in *Hagakure: The Book of the Samurai*, by Yamamoto Tsunetomo (translated by William Scott Wilson):

> **One who has never erred is dangerous.**

7

METHODOLOGICAL MINDFULNESS

> The Opposite of a Profound Truth
> is Another Profound Truth.

To have the Right Mindfulness you need the right methodology—Being ever mindful of the correct practice toward Enlightenment. Chapter 7 talks about methodologies and techniques. In the simplest analysis, a methodology is just an approach—a combined recipe, checklist and tutorial to help get through a project successfully. As with most things in life, the Middle Way is best: having no methodology, and slavishly following a methodology, are equally bad.

The Power of Babel

First we need to get a little terminology straight, since this is a case where there is a many-to-many relationship between terms and concepts, to use the vernacular. The bewildering variety of different terms used by various analysts and gurus impedes communication. In hopes of reducing the confusion, I've prepared the little chart below. You'll see how the different terms are used for the same thing and the same terms are used for different things. That's exactly what we Data Administrators keep telling everyone else they should never do! Oh well, as I keep telling you, there are many ways to the mountaintop; so I suppose we should stop being so sanctimonious about inconsistent data names throughout our systems.

Context	Category	Thing	2 Things	Fact	Behavior	Inheritance
CRC Cards	Class	N/A	Collaboration	(Attribute)	Responsibility	Superclass/Subclass
ERD	Entity Type	Entity	Relationship	Attribute	In DFD	Supertype/Subtype
Relational	Relation	Tuple	Foreign Key	Attribute	N/A	N/A
Database	Table	Row	Database Key	Column	Service, Procedure	3+ Variations
Programmer	Layout	Record	Pointer	Variable	Function	Base/Derived
UML	Class	Object	Association	Property	Method	Generalization
Etc., etc., etc…	Entity, Type, Structure, File	Occurrence, Instance	Pairing	Field, Item	Message, Operation, Algorithm, Trigger	Parent/Child, Is-a, Root/Branch/Leaf, General/Specific

At first I called the first column "camp" thinking the terminology set was associated with a group of people, but I later realized it also depended on context, as I caught myself using terms from the various camps throughout a Project's life cycle. For example, when you're referring to a database table it won't do to call it an entity, it's become a table.

I should say a few words here to mollify the Objective Orientalists (i.e., strict followers of Object Oriented methods) in the audience. You will no doubt be saying to yourself "Patrick's trying to say a class is just an entity in disguise". (Actually, I am, but I use this subterfuge to befuddle the O/O zealots—shh, don't tell them my secret). We need to make a distinction between classes that take advantage of the O/O programming mechanisms and those that are about the business. Many objects are not part of the problem domain, which is to say, the business user wouldn't recognize them. What you need to model is the business, so call the category business objects, or entity classes if you like. For data modeling, this is ALL you care about: the rest are just clutter. We are primarily concerned here with business objects, the classes we'll be looking at are entity objects, so I'll call them entities for short.

In truth Object Oriented methodologies might have been better named "Class Oriented", since we are typically focusing on classes, which are categories, and not objects, which are individual instances of the class. In C++, you use the keyword `class`, not the nonexistent keyword `object`, to use OOP features. Maybe they didn't want the acronym COP, which after all is better than Oops.

If you think this discussion confusing, you should attend one of my classes in C++programming that covers O/O classes. I use a school registration system as an example, in which one of the O/O classes represents a school class (as in a course), so find myself saying things like: "Now class, in this class, the Class class will be represented by this classy Class class." So I'm afraid I'm not convinced when I hear OO advocates say "Object Oriented is more like the way people think".

Religious Wars

A methodology can be too rigidly followed, in that the practice becomes the goal, which is usually unfortunate. Some consider a methodology to be Holy Writ, and some practitioners would sooner change their religion than their methodology. These people believe those who use the wrong methodology are not only mistaken, they're *evil*. I'm certainly not one of those people, and you shouldn't be, either—there are many paths to the mountaintop—and there is no one true methodology. Further, take a loose interpretation of what is required of a methodology—a methodology must be freely adaptable to the problem at hand.

The early Christian missionaries were pleased when they easily won converts among the Japanese, who then earnestly requested crucifixes to take home to keep in the place of highest honor. But they were shocked to discover the place of highest honor was right next to the statue of Buddha. The Japanese saw no conflict between the two religions and so had no problem being both Christian and Buddhist. If you ask a Japanese "Are you Shinto, Buddhist, Taoist or Confucian", the answer will probably be "Yes".

When it comes to methodologies, be like the Japanese. If a formal methodology is followed too strictly, it can become what Tom DeMarco & Timothy Lister's *Peopleware* calls a "Big M Methodology". They cite the example of a methodology that required an 18-part operator's manual, so the project team produced one, even though the device in question was going on a satellite and no one could "operate" it without going out in space. Ed Yourdon, a famous methodologist himself, in *Death March* speaks of techniques to circumvent the "Methodology Police", even recommending threatening to resign on the spot if forced to use a cumbersome methodology.

Karate is learned in three stages, called Shu-Ba-Ri. At first, the student must strictly follow forms (Shu) that minutely detail prescribed sequences of moves called *kata*. Each motion must always be conducted precisely according to the ancient ritual, and one's progress is evaluated based on how faithful one is to the form. Only after mastering the kata are you allowed to ignore (Ba) the exact sequences, experiment, and choose your own techniques. Eventually you are allowed to transcend the rules entirely (Ri), and develop your own strategy in complete freedom. This is a good way of looking at methodologies. When you are inexperienced, it's best to follow a methodology scrupulously. As Geoffrey James says in *The Tao of Programming*: "What is appropriate for the master is not appropriate for the novice. You must understand Tao before transcending structure." After a little experience, feel free to mix and match techniques, and skip steps as you see fit. When you've reached the higher level of Ri, you can develop your own techniques without regard to established methodologies, establishing your own methodology, even write a book on it!

No successful methodology absolutely requires every step be completed. But skipping any step brings risks that might be avoided. Beware the practice at many companies: "We never have time to do it right, but we always make time to do it over". Never break a rule out of ignorance, but rather after careful consideration of the situation. For some Research & Development projects a project plan is almost silly since you have no idea where you're going, when, or how. At the other extreme, in routine development, an established team can skip many of the steps. The key to successful shortening is constant vigilance to detect and correct problems as they develop.

Even writing a computer program follows this pattern. When you are first learning, you need to diagram, pseudocode, walkthrough, and perhaps even flowchart the simplest programs. When you have become an advanced programmer, you can skip these steps if you deem it safe. Eventually, you might have occasion to write high-performance code that completely violates all the usual rules of good programming.

Sashimi isn't SAD

In this section we'll compare the traditional method, unfortunately labeled SAD (Systems Analysis & Design), with a variation suggested by Nonaka & Takeuchi in The HBR article "The New New Product Development Game" which has come to be called the Sashimi approach. First let's consider the traditional methodology built around the SDLC—System Development Life Cycle, in combination with a Yourdonesque (Much of this methodology was developed and popularized by Ed Yourdon and his associates) Current Physical ➔ Current Logical ➔ New Logical ➔ New Physical analysis cycle as being "traditional Systems Analysis and Design" methods. This life cycle is often pictured as a waterfall, with the product of each phase cascading down to the phase below. Some see the diagram as a staircase or escalator; Those who see an escalator usually feel the escalator is running against them, not with them.

The cycle begins with a **feasibility study**, essentially just the step in which the project is approved; it ends with funding for the project, or at least for the next step. **Analysis** is where we figure out what the business problem is and what problems we need to solve, and we produce the *requirements* for the new system. In **design**, we decide how we will solve the problem, producing *specifications*, or *specs*. **Coding** produces the actual system, which we **test** rigorously, unless we're like Microsoft and leave all the testing to our customers. **Installation** will include training, data conversion, and software installation. New work rules will have to be implemented, and psychological resistance from the users will be at its height. So this phase might turn out to be the most critical of all—it's your last chance to really blow it, so don't give it short shrift.

Most OOAD advocates reject the waterfall, calling it part of the problem, not a solution. The Three Amigos, Ivar Jacobson, Grady Booch & James Rumbaugh, for example, describe the *Unified Software Development Process* in a book of the same name as Use-case driven, Architecture-Centric, Iterative, and Incremental (—quite a mouthful). The life cycle is variously pictured as a spiral (Hopefully, not a death spiral!), or a mandala, or a fountain, or a cycle within a cycle. No matter how you slice and dice the phases, though, the activities are the same. All experience all steps whether they admit it or not, but OOAD tends to emphasize a series of small steps (iterative & incremental) as opposed to the big sequential phases of the SDLC. The nature of O/O is that one object might be completely implemented before another is even started, so you might be doing parts of all the SDLC phases at any given moment. This parallelism is seen as a great advantage, and is believed to mitigate the Rayleigh effect seen in traditional projects with uneven staffing over the life cycle, rising as analysis and design crest, peaking with the coding phrase, and then dropping off for installation as the project wraps up and winds down.

This nonsequential approach is most typified by Nonaka & Takeuchi's Sashimi life cycle. Sashimi is a Japanese dish, similar to sushi but without the vinegrated rice. Sashimi cooks spend many years mastering cooking techniques, which seem deceptively simple since the cooking consists of NOT cooking the fish. In any event, the fish is usually sliced, and arranged on the plate with each slice stacked upon, and overlapping, the others. Likewise, system development phases can be stacked upon, and overlap, each other,

The successful new product development teams in the leading companies in Nonaka & Takeuchi's study had the following six characteristics:

1. Built-in instability. Teams were given broad goals or general strategic direction, not a clear-cut product or work plan. The teams had challenging goals, and great freedom, but no specifics. Paradoxically, ambiguity can be a great clarifier.

2. Self-organizing project teams. This requires autonomy, which means the team is truly empowered, with top management rarely intervening. By truly empowered, I don't mean the oft-used definition seen in many companies where empowerment is a buzzword: "You are empowered to make any decision, as long as it's the same decision I, the manager, would have made." The ideal manager has an open wallet and a closed mouth.

3. Overlapping development phases. As the Sashimi cycle shows, several, maybe even all, phases are proceeding simultaneously. This avoids the throw-it-over-the-wall syndrome that happens when an analysis team spends months developing requirements that are thrown over the wall to the design team that spends months developing specs that are thrown over the wall to the coding team.

4. Multilearning. Both multilevel and multifunctional learning must be encouraged. Individuals, teams, and the company as a whole should be encouraged to learn. And in keeping with Musashi's fourth dictum—Know the Ways of All Professions—you need to be open to learning from other fields. The most critical is technicians need to learn about business and economics, and nontechnical team members must learn technology.

5. **Subtle control.** If the team is to have autonomy, management must avoid the temptation to take direct control. Such tactics as balancing the team's members, tolerating mistakes, understanding the rhythm of the cycle, and encouraging direct customer contact can be used to subtly control the team's direction.

6. **Organizational transfer of learning.** In addition to the multilearning within the group, it is important the lessons they learn spread throughout the organization. One way to do this is by osmosis: disperse the members of the successful team among other teams to serve as examples.

Which is Methodology is Best?

As usual: "It Depends". The control system for a 500-passenger aircraft might need somewhat more rigor than a video rental system.

Stephen R. Schach in *Classical and Object-Oriented Software Engineering* finds the Waterfall model a more disciplined approach, achieved by the requirement to produce documentation at every step. The problem can be, to quote Schach: "In general, specification documents are long, detailed, and, quite frankly, boring to read". As a consequence, the delivered product may not meet the client's needs. He notes that iterative techniques characterized by Object Oriented methodologies have the advantage of incrementalism and parallelism, but warns they can degenerate into an undisciplined CABTAB (code a bit, test a bit) approach that might never meet the need, either.

In general, either approach can work, and either might be preferable depending on your staff and your project. If your staff is thoroughly familiar with and enthusiastic about a certain methodology, you might do well to use that approach unless project considerations preclude it. As to projects, large, well structured, familiar problems will probably succumb to traditional approaches, while small projects, and projects dealing with unstructured or groundbreaking advances will probably be better with Sashimi.

Brain Typhoon

Brainstorming is one of the most useful tools to stimulate creativity available to the Analyst. I use it almost daily in analysis and in all creative work. Brainstorming is a process you probably have done unconsciously, but it improves with some formal rules. I suggest you post them in a chart form in meeting rooms.

> 0. Have Fun!
> 1. No Criticism
> 2. No Self-Censorship
> 3. Piggyback

1. No Criticism

This is the most important rule of all. If someone offers the stupidest idea you ever heard in your life, the correct response is to say, "Fantastic!" Under no circumstances do you want to stop the creative flow by intimidating anyone. Some of the craziest ideas you've ever heard turn out to work once given a chance. But more important, a dumb idea can flow into another better idea if you give it a chance.

2. No Self-Censorship

This is almost as important. Don't hold back. If you think of the stupidest thing you've ever heard of in your life, blurt it out. Sometimes you are able to come up with an idea which is completely absurd, except that it works—because you look at a problem from the odd perspective— you "think different". This often lets you attack a difficult problem from another angle, one that leads to a surprisingly elegant solution. Even if it isn't adopted, it might start someone else thinking, or at a minimum will get a laugh and help to loosen up the group.

3. Piggyback

Hey, for once in life stealing is okay, in fact encouraged. Try to modify or expand on the ideas offered by the other participants. And if someone steals your idea, remember those who see farther are standing on the shoulders of giants, and that means you're a giant. Ideas feed on other ideas, and piggyback is not only okay, it's admirable. You want to take every idea to its illogical conclusion.

0. Have Fun

Although this one appears first on my chart, I have PowerPoint animated to have it appear last when I'm explaining the rules to a group. I explain that as a C++programmer I naturally count from zero, not one. This rule is first because I've found that groups that are having fun usually do the best job.

I often use a silly brainstorming exercise as an icebreaker, a way to loosen a group of people up, especially if they don't know each other. You might consider something similar for a meeting of a new group, especially if you will be using brainstorming and need to warm up. Explain brainstorming, form the group into teams of four to eight people, and then pose a silly problem to the group, such as this one I often pose at my UC Berkeley Extension class:

> Berkeley is in a terrible fix. With the rainy season approaching, we decided to put coat racks and hangers in all the classrooms and offices. It seems a new employee went on to CoatHangers.com on the Internet, and like many UI's, this one was confusing, so she accidentally ordered not the 5,000 hangers wanted, but 5,000 cases of hangers, with

10,000 hangers in each case. There is no way to cancel this order. Your mission is to come up with as many possible uses for these hangers to get Cal out of this jam.

If asked "what kind of hangers, wood or wire?" Tell them "Every imaginable kind". This further opens the road to thought. You can vary the problem by using just about any item, although I tried it once with clothespins and it didn't work very well. Some of the students didn't know what a clothespin was!

Without telling them what I'm doing, I tally the number of times I hear laughter coming from each group. When we get to the reward phase (see below) the first behavior I reward is the "Fun Group", the one that laughed the most. In many learning situations, noise equals learning. For my course on systems analysis consulting, I consider the number of times the neighboring classes complain about the noise an indicator of how well things are going.

> ### The Goal of Brainstorming is Quantity not Quality

Quality will come from the process. The point of the exercise, and of brainstorming, is to generate as many ideas as you can. With more options, you are more likely to come up with a good solution. It's easier to cross out the bad ideas than to come up with good ones.

The process

1. Brainstorm

Discuss the rules, and perhaps do an icebreaker, such as the hanger exercise, or any from the *Games Trainers Play* series of books. Someone needs to be the scribe, and record all the ideas on a white board or flip chart. If your session is facilitated, the facilitator will be the scribe, and not participate. So just have the people shout the ideas out, with the caveat the scribe(s) need time to record them. With all meetings, especially free wheeling sessions with lots of ideas and decisions, this rule applies:

> **If it ain't recorded,
> It didn't happen.**

2. Reward

The next step is to reward the best performers. The reward can be a cheap gag toy, some candy, or just a pat on the back. In my class, the students in the rewarded groups get an extra point toward their final grade. All students receive one point for participating in the class exercise, plus each student gets an extra point for each category they "won" in. Often one group wins in more than one category—the fun group especially seems to win in one or both of the other categories.

These are the categories rewarded: 1. Most Fun—the group that laughed the most. 2. Most Ideas—the group with the greatest total number of ideas. 3. Most Bizarre, Strange or Ridiculous—the group with craziest idea. Note you should **NOT** reward the *best* idea, nor the one that is eventually chosen to work on. The best idea arises from the process, and everyone was part of that. This is to encourage the correct behavior. If you want people to think out of the box, reward them for escaping.

3. Reality Check

Now reality must raise its ugly head. If your boss has said, "Under no circumstances will you go to Hawai'i", then Hawai'i, alas, must be cut from the list. If you're doing brainstorming right, you will have come up with some things that are just plain impossible. But remember, what seems quite absurd can in fact be quite feasible. After all, if the infrastructure weren't built, the idea of the ubiquitous automobile would seem absurd. Not just to make the autos themselves, requiring materials from all over the world, but consider the requirements: You must build a ribbon of concrete from every place to every other place, with gas stations strategically located dispensing oil that comes from deep under ground in the far corners of the planet. It will never work! So only remove ideas that are patently absurd, illegal or clearly impossible given company policy or politics.

4. Clean the List Up

Categorize and combine items. By classifying them on some characteristic (brainstorm a list…), you'll find the same idea appears twice, or will see a hole or a whole. Try fusion and fission: some ideas combine, some split into two. Combine any two ideas that are the same, or split any cases where two ideas are posing as one.

5. Select

Hopefully you will have more ideas than you can possibly work on. So how to decide which merit further investigation? There are essentially three ways:

Autocracy—Some expert or authority shall decree the answer. Perhaps your assignment has been to come up with alternatives, not recommendations, and so you can pass the problem to the boss.

Democracy—or a modification of it. You could simply vote, or better, use a variation called *multi-voting*. In multi-voting, it's a weighted democracy, because each person gets multiple votes. How many? Usually three or four votes, but sometimes a good number is the number of alternatives you want to narrow down to. If you plan to look at six alternatives, you might give each participant six votes. Votes can be "blocked", i.e. you can cast several votes for the same choice, even cast all your votes on one choice if you really feel strongly about it. Multi-voting avoids several problems. Sometimes a lot of people are mildly in favor of an idea but a smaller number are very enthusiastic about another choice. Their enthusiasm can be registered by extra votes. Sometimes everybody's second choice is the best answer, which would be missed if everyone got only one vote.

Consensus—this involves getting broad agreement. It is covered in Chapter 3 on Consulting. Consensus is preferable when the success of the decision depends on cooperation and coordination.

Brainstorming works for either a group or an individual. Use it alone, use it with friends. Use it whenever you need to think out a problem or generate alternatives.

Naturally Normal

With Zen Analysis, you don't need normalization. E.F. Codd of IBM originated the concept of Normalization. Normalization has fallen out of favor, or at least fashion, in current practice. The Object Oriented design movement seems to have left normalization behind; I've seen dozens of O/O books, and I recall none even mentioning it. The Three Amigos (Booch, Rumbaugh and Jacobson—the inventors of UML) don't cover it in any of their comprehensive tomes. In academe, Database textbooks usually do cover normalization, and three leading Systems Analysis & Design textbooks I checked (Hoffer at al, Kendall & Kendal, and Whitten) include coverage, but four Software Engineering textbooks (Sommerville, Hamlet, van Vliet, and Braude) do not, despite the fact good software engineering requires a normal database. One database design author, Robert J. Muller, *Database Design for Smarties: Using UML for Data Modeling*, even rants about it, calling it an unnecessary ritual, saying some DBAs "insist on going though the stages of normalization and arguing Talmudic points along the way. Pilpul aside, (I had to look this one up in an unabridged dictionary. Pilpul is

Aramaic (Hebrew) and means a dispute over subtle details, especially in the Talmud.) normalization is a ritual, and often not a particularly useful one".

Most normalizers strive for third normal form (3NF). There are also three further normal forms, 4NF and 5NF, and Boyce-Codd, which falls between 3NF and 4NF: 3½NF?). In this discussion we'll limit ourselves to 3NF, which is sufficient for any real-world database you're likely to encounter, and because they are usually beyond the ken of even the most advanced Zen master. To be in third normal form (3NF), a relation must be in second normal form, and have no transitive dependencies. So what does *that* mean?

The various normal forms build on one another: to be in 3NF you must first be in 2NF, and to be in 2NF you must first be in 1NF. So what's first normal form? To be in 1NF, you need to have a key, which is a unique identifier, present in every tuple (A tuple is a fancy word for row, which I avoid because I can't decide whether to pronounce it tuhpul or too-pul, as in Tupelo, Mississippi). All attributes should be dependent on this key, so your relation cannot be just a random assortment of attributes. Technically, all relational databases are in 1NF, although they can fail to be in 1NF logically. For example, I've seen a "database" that was one table containing an exact image of the records that had existed in the predecessor flat file with all its redundancies and inconsistencies intact. There also must be no repeating groups (i.e. no attribute may have multiple values). For example, if an employee has multiple assignments, this relation is technically, but not logically 1NF:

EMPLOYEE (<u>SSN</u>, Assignment1, Assignment2, Assignment3)

Although Assignment1, Assignment2 and Assignment3 don't repeat in exact name, they repeat the same attribute logically and therefore will cause problems, and violate 1NF in spirit (so they are not "spiritually"

1NF?). By definition, the real-world Assignment is not dependent on SSN because one SSN can yield several different Assignments.

The next level, 2NF, is only a concern when there is a composite key. A relation violates this form when an attribute is dependent on a subset of the key, for example in a two-part key the attribute might be dependent on only one of the components of the key. Again, it's possible to be technically in 2NF although not logically. Some DBA's assign an arbitrary key to every relation, which is either randomly or sequentially generated. Since this is a single attribute key, all relations are technically in compliance with 2NF. In this case, if there is an obvious candidate key that violates the 2NF rules the relation has qualified for 2NF on a technicality and so probably shouldn't be called 2NF. In other words, don't get into 2NF by simply using an arbitrary device to eliminate the compound key.

So finally we get to the defining requirement needed for 3NF: "no transitive dependencies". Transitive dependencies are dependencies among the attributes. So no attribute may be dependent on any attribute of the relation except the key and any candidate keys. It's called transitive because the attribute's dependency on the key is transferred through its dependency on the nonkey attribute.

So, the oath of the Third Normal designer:

> I solemnly swear:
> Each attribute will depend on
> The key, (1NF)
> The whole key, (2NF)
> And nothing but the key (3NF)
> So help me Codd!

But normalization is important for entities and relational databases, and is at least twice as important for objects, as not only attributes, but also operations, need to be normalized. So how do thoroughly modern designers survive without it? Muller asserts that "it is very easy to put your database into fifth normal form with a simple, direct design." Although I don't agree fully with Mr. Muller's ranting (perhaps he was frightened by a DBA as a young child), Zen analysts are usually "Naturally Normal": if you carefully identify the entities (objects) in your system, and put the attributes with the entity they logically relate to, you'll be nicely normal even without going through the "ritual" of normalization. The normalization ritual can help clarify thinking and avoid many errors. Doing a normalization review requires you consider every individual attribute, why it's there and what it does. Such a painstaking review, although tedious, can pay off by uncovering mistakes, even many unrelated to normalization as such. So you can in fact achieve the same result using other techniques instead such as:

Patterns	as per the Gang of Four: Erich Gamma, Richard Helm, Ralph Johnson & John Vlissides, *Design Patterns: Elements of Reusable Object-Oriented Software.*
Heuristics	as per Arthur J. Riel *Object-Oriented Design Heuristics.*
Refactoring	as per Martin Fowler, *Refactoring: Improving the Design of Existing Code.*
Zen Analysis	as per Patrick McDermott, *Zen and the Art of Systems Analysis.*

Naturally, the last method is the best.

8

MEDITATIONS ON A MODEL

Good modeling often requires the Right Meditation. Chapter 8 delves into the most important analytical skill: the ability to abstract complex systems and build models to understand, explain and design systems. We'll look primarily at the nuts and bolts (actually the boxes & lines) of data models as we ponder the quintessence of Classes, Entities, Attributes and Relationships. In the process we'll answer some koans presented as guides to the truth.

Zen meditates on the relationship of perception to reality and concludes life is an illusion. This is true of models, as Craig Larman illustrates on the cover for his book *Applying UML and Patterns*, which echoes René Magritte's painting *Ceci n'est pas une pipe*. Magritte shows us a painting of a pipe that is so realistic as to appear from a distance to be a three-dimensional model, and warns us: *"This is not a pipe"*. Larman shows us a data model of a sailboat and warns us "This is not a sailboat". The data model is not the computer system, and the goal is not to build a model, it's to build a system, so don't mimic Pygmalion of Greek mythology. Pygmalion sculpted a model of his ideal woman. Unfortunately, he then found himself in love with the model, and no real woman could please him. Don't make Pygmalion your role model, unless you have a goddess friend called Aphrodite who can turn the model into reality for you like Pygmalion did.

The Sound of One Hand Clapping

In Zen Buddhism, an acolyte is given an essentially unanswerable puzzle, called a *kōan* (pronounced Koe AHN), to ponder on the way to enlightenment. One of the most famous koans is one created by Rinzai Zen master Hakuin (1686-1769) that goes like this: "You know the sound of two hands clapping—But what is the sound of *one* hand clapping?" Many questions in systems analysis are like Zen koans. Some of the conundrums we analysts face every day:

1. How Can You See What Cannot Be Seen?
2. How Many Words Is One Picture Worth?
3. What is The Ultimate Data Model?
4. What Should One Model?
5. When Is a Fact About a Thing In Fact a Thing?
6. Is There Organization Object Ontology?
7. What Is the Metaphysics of Metadata?
8. This can become so confusing you might even ask:
   "Who Am I?"

In many cases analysts talk a lot to answer little, like an incandescent bulb generating much more heat than light, but there is often more at stake than minutia and esoterica. Simply putting an attribute at the wrong level of a hierarchy of entities can be an incredibly expensive error, and these seemingly endless and random ruminations can prevent that. One of the intriguing aspects of analysis is this necessity to understand the quintessence of the situation, so we'll look at these analysis koans as a way of enlightenment.

Oh, yes, the sound of one hand clapping. If you're a systems analyst, you're probably already familiar with it without even realizing it. Here's how to hear it: First, if you're wearing glasses, remove them. Then extend your hand out, palm up. Vigorously hit your forehead with the palm of your hand. The smack you hear is the sound of one hand clapping.

1. How Can You See What Cannot Be Seen?

Musashi tells us we must perceive what cannot be seen as his seventh principle. The primary method used by analysts to see the unseen is the model. So before we understand our koan, we need to know what a model is. Models are a critical component of the Systems Analyst's toolkit. I can't imagine how to design a database without data models to visualize the relationships, although some people still do it without them. A model is just an abstraction of a part of the world. Models serve many purposes outside systems analysis. Fashion models allow consumers to visualize, or perhaps fantasize, what they might look like in designer clothes. Budgets are models that allow managers to visualize, or perhaps fantasize, how project spending might unfold. Business models allow entrepreneurs to visualize, or perhaps fantasize, how they might make money.

A model can be one of three things. It can be a *representation* of something. Data models help understand the structure and connections of data so a useful database can be conceptualized. A model can be a *pattern* for something to be made. Prototypes are models that allow users to describe how the eventual computer system should function so programmers can use them as a pattern for the system. A model can be an *analogy* or description used to help see something not normally seen. Rutherford developed a model to describe atomic structure. Mathematical models let economists and meteorologists predict events. Okay, green tea leaves are usually better predictors than econometric and meteorological models, but you get the idea.

Many of our models will be pictures or diagrams, allowing us to visualize the process and experiment with it before actually implementing it. But models are not always visual. Econometric models are systems of mathematical equations. And the use case models used in UML are more text-based than visual, but they are models nonetheless—models of interactions between people and computers. In fact, a computer program is a model, and a database is, too.

Some caveats are in order. An important point: most models simplify the object they portray, and will not be exact representations of the real world. A good model will highlight what we are interested in, but hide what we are not. It is usually cheaper and safer to manipulate a model than it is to manipulate real world objects.

Models are only valuable for the purpose they serve; they have no intrinsic worth. I once took over a project that had been in analysis (not psychoanalysis, though that might have been appropriate) for about two years, and had produced many pages of circles, boxes and arrows. There were circles, boxes and arrows on boards; circles, boxes and arrows on the walls; and especially circles, boxes and arrows in binders—but no system, and not even one program. A classic case of analysis paralysis, the time had long passed to just do it. Once again, you must seek the Middle Way. The model should receive enough effort to fulfill its purpose, and no more. If your goal is to explain, cut unnecessary detail. If it is ephemeral, don't put too much effort into it.

2. How Many Words is One Picture Worth?

The saying is "A picture's worth a thousand words", but that is not true. It can be a gross understatement. The file that contains a typical picture is about 500,000 bytes, which means it could easily hold a hundred thousand English words. Try to write a "word picture"—Describe, using words alone, the woodblock from Hokusai's *36 Views of Mount Fuji*. For someone to actually reproduce the woodblock from words without having seen it even 100,000 words would not suffice. And a scan of a page usually requires many more bytes than the text on it. (Incidentally, Hokusai is an early case of scope creep—there are actually are more than 36 views in the series *36 Views of Mount Fuji*.)

Which better conveys an idea, words or pictures? Embrace contradiction: choose the right tool—the answer is "It depends". For a high-level overview, you can't beat a diagram, but eventually diagrams aren't appropriate. They become too complex and don't illustrate desired system functions. For example, trying to show every decision point and path in a program will simply result in a line of tangles similar to a photo of the wires and cables behind your desk.

Flowcharting detailed program logic is an example of a picture of little value. Assume a system in which we need to process all the Items for a given Order. A flowchart of a loop statement requires a diagram with four boxes, a diamond and five lines, but the code itself looks like this:

```
int Counter=0;
while (Counter++< ItemCount)
      ValidateItem();
```

The flowchart diagram is much larger than the statements themselves, and doesn't translate directly into code in any event. The flowchart can be a teaching tool to get the concept of the loop or if statement across to novices, but after that it is of no value.

The Microsoft Access ® Query builder feature surprisingly enough doesn't even work well for teaching. I at first thought this feature would help students who had no programming background grasp Boolean concepts. Logical and's and or's and not's, are difficult to grasp and explain, and I thought this visual approach would be helpful. Instead of grasping the actual SQL code, that looks like this:

```
SELECT Name, City, State, CreditLimit
    FROM Customer
    WHERE (City="Oakland" OR City="Redmond") OR
    (State="CA" AND CreditLimit>1000) OR
    CreditLimit>10000;
```

They could visualize it on the Select Query screen with the criteria neatly arranged in order and no clumsy syntax to confuse them.

Surprisingly, neither of these representations was any easier to grasp than the other. Any student who could understand the Access query could understand the SQL and vice versa. If they didn't understand it one way, they didn't understand it the other way, either. The complexity was in understanding the *concepts*, not visualizing them. In models, attributes are best conveyed as lists, and even visual color-coding doesn't seem to help. And so with flow charts, decision trees and decision tables, the picture is not worth any words.

> **A Picture is Worth 100,000 Words**
> **—or Zero**

3. What is The Ultimate Data Model?

The ultimate universal data model is a box labeled "Thing" with a many-to-many optional recursive relationship. Every thing is a thing, and so only one entity type is needed. And as the First Law of Ecology tells us, everything is related to everything else.

That's one extreme. At the other extreme, everything is unique, and thus needs to be a unique entity unto itself. One of the realizations of the Tao is that no day is like any other: each day, although similar in many ways to those that went before and will come after, is nonetheless absolutely unique. Every day is unique, every snowflake is unique, and especially every person is unique. We must, however, be able to classify things based on similarities and differences if we are ever to use a computer effectively. Everything is the same, yet everything is distinct. The best answer lies somewhere between these extremes. And so once again we must choose The Middle Way.

4. What Should One Model?

This is probably the most important tip in this book. If it works in the world, it has to work in your system, but if it does not work that way in the world, it probably won't work in the system. Remember the Third Law of Ecology: Nature knows Best. Zen honors Nature. Your representation is most likely to be right if it models the working real world analog as closely as possible. It will also help you and others understand it and find it when you're looking for it months later. All of the indexing, cross-referencing and searching won't be as good as having it be in its logical place. It's also the easiest representation to understand, assuming you understand the world, which you have to do anyway.

> Model the World

Use this as your analysis tool: Go look at the world. The computer system is a model of the business. So, for example, if the business is recording and tracking certain data, then your computer system needs to do so, too. For an example of a real world/machine analog, there must be an Entity (or group of entities) if:

There's a form. Forms are expensive to design and make. So if the business designed a form they definitely are recording information that should be kept as well in your machine analog. A good analyst always collects forms that are being used by anyone she interviews. Be sure to get some completed examples. Look for stray marks indicating status or type. The name of the entity might not be obvious: A packing slip represents a shipment; a receipt represents a payment.

Sections and boxes on forms also often enclose an entity. There is often a bold line marking off sections; each section could hide an entity.

There are several copies. Look for multiple part forms, especially with copies of different colors. Go to an office supply store and look at some of the forms. Carbon or carbonless paper is used to make multiple copies of invoices, receipts, orders, etc.

There's a file. If there is a Claims File, the odds are there will be a Claim entity. If there are filing cabinets in the office ask, "What files are in here?" The answer will be the name of an entity you need in your system.

There's a serial number. Objects have identities. If they've given something an identity, it *is* an entity. Serial numbers, prenumbered forms all indicate an entity.

It's important. Things the business considers important must be tracked.

In addition as its use as an analysis tool, "Model the World" is important as a design rule. If it doesn't work that way in the world, watch out! It can be dangerous to ignore the rule. The underlying problem is demonstrated by an address change after a move. The last time I moved, I sent my bank a change of address notice, and soon enough my checking account statements began arriving like clockwork at the new address. But my savings account, credit card, IRA, and CD continued to be sent to the old address. It took three change-of-address forms to actually get all of my accounts going to the new address. This was because I was apparently in their system three different times. Since there is only one of me, they didn't model the world.

I'm encouraged if I have a conflict in my model and discover it holds in the world—it means we are accurate. There is often a conflict in the model between people and the roles they play. This models real world as anyone involved in an office romance knows, and anyone juggling parenthood and employment. The roles conflict. It is complex in the real world so if it models world it might also conflict, and that shouldn't make you uncomfortable because that means it is accurate.

O/O Analysis sometimes goes off the track with its emphasis on messages sent between objects. There are no messages. One thing making O/O not helpful is this confusion, especially in Java where everything is an object. A number format, for example, is not an object in the real world, but it is in Java. C++is superior in this regard because it is a hybrid, and supports both objects and procedures. Arthur J. Riel in *Object-Oriented Design Heuristics* has a rule: "Model the real world *whenever possible*". (Italics added). He then allows: "This heuristic is often violated for reasons of system intelligence distribution, avoidance of god classes, and the keeping of related behavior and data in one place." I would argue even these are rarely good reasons to ignore the rule:

Systems Intelligence? You're more intelligent than Mother Nature? It's not nice to fool Mother Nature…

Avoiding god classes? If the real gods thought there was a god class, why shouldn't you?

Keeping related behavior in one place? Related in whose mind? Not the gods, not the world, not the users…

What if the business does not faithfully reflect the real world? The Dot.coms showed this was a real possibility. But that's a different problem—Don't update the model, update your résumé.

5. When is a Fact About a Thing In Fact a Thing?

A computer systems' most important function is to keep track of things: customers, bills and payments; students, teachers and courses; citizens, taxes and refunds—computers keep track of all these things. But you need a place to keep the data, and how to do that? There are three categories of data we keep in traditional data modeling: entities, relationships and attributes (ERA). Object Oriented analysis adds behavior, referred to as Methods, and uses different terminology; so classes, relationships, attributes and methods (CRAM), with classes corresponding to entities, at least during business analysis. An *entity* is just "A *Thing* the Business needs to know about". Since that's not too helpful, I've found "Entity" is best defined by examples. Entities can be people, places, or things. They can be events, roles, or organizations. They can even be other systems. Entities are tangible or intangible, and even conceptual such as a cost center or account. And they can be collections of other objects. So they can be just about anything the business cares about. A *relationship* is a connection of some kind between two objects that is significant to the business. And an *attribute* is a fact about an entity. One of the trickiest problems in analysis is determining which of these categories a piece of data falls into. For example: "Is X an entity or an attribute?" Is it a fact about a thing (and thus an attribute) or in fact a thing (in which case its an entity)?

Try this one. Is a telephone number an attribute, an entity, or a relationship? By now you can guess the answer is: It Depends. For most applications, it will be an attribute, which is what most people answer. But to the phone company, a number not only isn't a mere attribute, it isn't even just an entity—it's at least three entities. In North America, phone numbers have three distinct parts: my number is (510)893-2943. The first part (510), as you probably know, is called the area code. Everyone knows what the other two parts are, but not many know what they're called. They are the Exchange (893) and the Subscriber number

(2943). To the phone company, the area code, exchange, and subscriber number are each important entities in themselves. For the area code, they need to track the location, whether it is public or private, whether it is toll, toll-free, or regular, and so on. For the exchange, they need its location, the PBX if any, and so forth. And for the subscriber number, they need the address, billing information, etc.

Telephone numbers in Japan are one of those quaint things Japanese. I say "things Japanese" as an allusion to Basil Hall Chamberlain's 1905 book *Things Japanese*, which was inexplicably renamed *Japanese Things* by Charles E. Tuttle Company in their 1971 reprint. Tuttle is usually very simpatico with their specialized audience and authors, but this is an example of a failure to understand the intent of an author: "Japanese Things" ain't got the ring. Despite Tuttle's rare lapse, it's a great book. Read it! But I digress.

Japan has a surprisingly irrational phone system. To get a telephone connection, you have to tell the telephone company what the telephone number will be. No kidding, the telephone company has no telephone numbers. You have to buy a number from someone; some numbers are very expensive, and others very cheap. For example, the number four can be pronounced "shi", which also means "death". So a number with a lot of fours is a bad number indeed, and cheap. Eight, on the other hand, means "wealth", so only a wealthy person could afford all eights. The Japanese language has a limited number of possible syllables, and multiple pronunciations for most words, including numbers, one from aboriginal Japanese and one from Chinese, so it's usually easy to make a phrase out of a number, like vanity license plates in the US. Clever phrases are worth a lot. This system apparently dates back to the original phone system in the 1920s. Politicians were given blocks of phone numbers in return for favorable votes, bureaucrats for favorable decisions; since no money or property was involved it didn't meet the definition of a bribe. But now no one who owns an expensive number wants to end the system.

There is no easy rule to determine whether to use an attribute or an entity, but I'll give some guidelines that I've found helpful. After a while, you'll get a Zen-like ability to know instantly, but it's a hard distinction to explain.

We sometimes use **Grammatical Analysis** to determine which category information belongs in. Entities or Classes are usually Nouns; Relationships are Verbs; Attributes are Adjectives; and Methods are Phrases, including an action and a class, relationship, attribute or a combination thereof.

Next is the "**Of Test**". Attributes are "OF" a class. If you can't make sense of the data without an 'of', it's an attribute. Name? Name of what? Name of the Employee, so Name is an attribute of Employee. Date? Date of what? Date of Receipt of Invoice, so Date is an attribute of Invoice.

Attributes have no attributes. When is an Attribute not an Attribute? When it has an attribute itself. Attributes do not have attributes. If there's a fact about it, it's an entity, if not, it's an attribute. Watch out for the multi-value attribute, particularly for a status (e.g. customer status and invoice status).

6. Is there Organization Object Ontology?

What is the ontology of organizations? Ontology is said to be "the study of the nature of being and existence", but my extensive research has convinced me it's actually Greek for "You'll get a headache if you think about this very long". So in this section we'll study the nature of being an organization until we understand, or get a headache, whichever comes first. Our organizations deal with many external organizations and they must be represented in our data models. The rule for data models is simple, based on Albert Einstein's dictum concerning models in Physics:

> **Make it as simple as it can be,
> but no simpler.**

You'd think that would be easy, but it is surprisingly difficult to get a model of organizations that has as much detail as is needed, but no more than can be reasonably maintained. There are actually three parts to this problem. (Actually there is a fourth, but I can only remember three of them at any one time.) The first is we deal with both organizations and people, second they play many roles, and third the computer cannot resolve variations in addresses.

First, a customer or a vendor might be an *organization* such as a corporation, firm, or government agency, or it could be a living, breathing human being. You need to keep different data, or at least structure it differently, depending on which it is. An organization name is just a name, but a person's name has parts: first, middle and last name. It is difficult to tease these out of an unstructured field. You also will keep different attributes and relationships for organizations and people. Customers and vendors might be either real live people, or else companies or other organizations. Silverston, Inmon & Graziano in *The Data Model Resource Book*, and David C. Hay in *Data Model Patterns*, both recommend the approach of subtyping *Party* into *Organization* and *Person*.

The next problem is that of *roles*. The same party, to use the terminology of the two books, can play many roles. A vendor or an employee might also be a customer, for example. Consider the baffling variety of roles outside organizations can have with Amazon.com. One person or company might play many of these roles at the same or different times. Let's take a high-level look at the parties involved in Amazon.com's business:

Associate: An associate links eyeballs from an outside website, and gets paid a commission when a purchase is made by the customer who followed the link.

Authorized Merchant: includes zShops and auctioneers. Amazon serves as an agent, and collects and transmits the money, less a fee for the service.

Author: In addition to writing the book, the author provides content, such as reviews and interviews.

Bank: Makes ePayments.

Carrier: UPS, USPS, FedEx. Responsible for the delivery; Amazon sometimes will receive a tracking number which is given to the customer via Email and recorded as part of the order status.

Credit Card: MasterCard, Visa, AmEx, etc. Credit card companies are the main source of money income, as most purchases are paid for with credit cards.

Customer: The consumer. Gets order fulfillment information and promotions (ads and coupons). Customers write reviews, and provide other content such as recommendation lists.

Distributor: Supplies the product, but doesn't make it—either imports or warehouses it. Might send direct in the cases of trusted distributors, but usually sends the items to Amazon for re-shipment. For books, traditional book distributors, such as Ingrams are crucial to Amazon' business.

Honor System Member: Users to their website decide to pay the member on the honor system. Amazon will collect and transmit payments. Honor system member is charged 15¢ per transaction plus 15% of the payment amount.

Manufacturer: Makes an item Amazon.com sells. Might or might not supply it to Amazon.com, could co-brand or co-advertise, or pay for placement at the top of the search list.

Publisher: Publishes the books. Note Manufacturer and Publisher fill the same role.

"**Trusted Partner**": Amazon.com sends eyeballs, and must track them. In addition to the products they sell, Amazon has teamed with Toys R Us and CarsDirect.com to sell toys and automobiles, for example. They can apparently cover some of the costs of advertising and website development by steering customers to these other companies, turning technology into a revenue-producing product.

Vendor/Supplier: Supplies items that are needed for business, not for re-sale.

Warehouse: Amazon warehouses, the critical component in order fulfillment. Fills the order, sends shipping information to the carrier for pickup. Some book distributors effectively fill this role.

In a traditional design, each role would be represented as a different entity type and eventually database table, so a party filling many roles would appear in the database many times. We can separate the parties from the roles to avoid this redundancy, but at a cost in complexity.

The third problem is that of *address variations.* You will easily recognize that XYZ Company is both a vendor and a company even though the attention line on the address is "Ann Pollywog, Accounts Payable" and the other is "Alvin Richards, Accounts Receivable" but to the computer they are different addresses and have to be tracked differently. Say a company is both a vendor and a customer. In all probability they will be different at the bit and byte level, to wit, you'll be dealing with the accounts payable department on the customer side and the accounts receivable on the vendor side. The ATTN: line will be different, the department name will be different; in some companies even the city will be different. So are they the same organizations and thus the same entity? Since one of the goals of a single entity is to change both addresses at the same time this might not work, since one address might change and the other not. This is going a step further than my bank problem, i.e. in a single role I want all addresses the same (maybe). I want checking, savings, CD, IRA all to change at the same time and kept in sync.

Now unfortunately this is indeed an inherently complex problem. If you're not confused, you haven't been paying attention. Silverston et al. solve it with a data model that requires 12 entity types plus 5 subtypes and 18 relationships! For something that is sometimes tracked as a single entity type. Is it really worth it? It probably won't save space because overhead of entities and relationships will probably outweigh the redundant data. And it's pretty complex, so programmers will make errors and users will make errors so you'll probably be worse off anyway.

Since Silverston is indeed correct in his model, why doesn't it work well? Computers aren't smart enough. Even a bored distracted clerk will identify two similar but slightly different addresses as the same; computers cannot yet make these simple distinctions, requiring manual intervention to make the judgment. And programmers aren't smart enough. Even though most humans deal with these problems every day and don't even see them as a problem, programming them has been impossible up until now. Perhaps someday AI will advance to a point this will no longer be true, but until then, the Systems Analyst is the key player in making systems successful.

7. What is the Metaphysics of Metadata

Data & Metadata

Metadata is surely a Zen-like concept, truly metaphysical. The *meta*-part of metaphysics is from the Greek, meaning "beyond" or "transcending", and the *physics* as in physical. In a 1569 collection of Aristotle, the works on the nature of being (ontology), space (cosmology) and knowing (epistemology) were sequenced after the works on physical topics, so were beyond physics, or "metaphysics". It was apt, since these subjects were also beyond physics intellectually, and the name stuck.

The *meta* prefix has been applied to subjects like linguistics, where a metalanguage is a language about languages. Metadata uses this sense, in that metadata is "data about data"—definitional data about tables, records, and other data structures, attributes or fields and their types, domains, etc. It's information about the nature of the data to be kept, rather than the data itself. The distinction between data and metadata is especially important because most IT Departments are organized so that the applications programmers and DBAs (Data Base Administrators) are in different reporting lines, often even reporting up to different Vice Presidents. The data is in the realm of programmers and users, while the Data Administrators and DBAs are responsible for the metadata. So if the customer's name is misspelled, it's a data problem and the user should fix it. If the customer's name is missing, it's a data integrity problem and the programmer should fix the program to require the name. If the field will only accept a two-character name, it's a metadata problem and the DBA should fix it. If the customer's name is kept in incompatible format in different records, it's the data administrator's problem.

Metaphysical can be a derogatory term meaning abstract abstruse, or subtle, and surely many data administrators have been justly accused of that. Metadata, like metaphysics, involves exploring the relation between mind and matter, substance and attribute, fact and value. It is concerned with the fundamental nature of reality and being—some metadata and metaphysical discussions will sometimes be indistinguishable.

I was once at a DAMA conference where someone had a sheet of music and someone jokingly referred to it as "metamusic". On reflection, though, I realized that was not the appropriate name, since the sheet music was about music whereas metamusic should be music about music. So *The Tennessee Waltz* would be a metasong. The words tell of another dance at another time when the singer "was dancing with my darling to the *Tennessee Waltz*", so this is a song about another song. *Begin the Beguine* is even clearer, since the song is a swing and the Beguine is a Tropical Waltz. Other metasongs are *The Land of 1,000 Dances* and *Blame it on the Bossa Nova*.

Database languages, such as SQL, recognize this distinction by having a DDL (Data Definition Language) to CREATE and DROP TABLES and other objects; and DML (Data Manipulation Language) to SELECT, INSERT, UPDATE, and DELETE rows in tables. Most DBAs will jealously defend their right to exclusively maintain the metadata. Observe what is covered in SQL.

DDL

```
CREATE TABLE TEACHER
(
    SSN        char(11) NOT NULL,
    LastName   char(20),
    FirstName  char(15),
    Street     char(35),
    City       char(20),
    State      char(2),
    Zip        char(5),
    Phone      char(11),
    Rate       INT,

    PRIMARY KEY(SSN)
);

CREATE TABLE COURSE
(
    ID          char(11) NOT NULL,
    Title       char(20),
    Units       char(15),
```

```
      HSorCollege      char(2),

      PRIMARY KEY(ID)
);

CREATE TABLE SESSION
(
      ID               char(11) NOT NULL,
      StartDate        char(8),
      EndDate          char(8),
      Time             char(25),
      Site             char(12),
      TeacherSSN       char(11),
      CourseID         char(11),

      PRIMARY KEY(ID),
      FOREIGN KEY(TeacherSSN) REFERENCES TEACHER(SSN),
      FOREIGN KEY(CourseID) REFERENCES COURSE(ID)
);
```

DML

```
   INSERT INTO Teacher
      VALUES ('123-45-6789',
            'McDermott','Patrick',
            'PO Box 20689',
            'Oakland','CA','94620',
            '893-1234',
            125);
   INSERT INTO Course
      VALUES ('MS666',
            'PHP, SQL & HTML',
```

```
      3,
      'C');
INSERT INTO Session
   VALUES ('SS8833B1',
      '1/1/03',
      '1/31/03',
      'M - F 9:00 - 12:00',
      'Bernal',
      '123-45-6789',
      'MS666');
```

HTML meta tags also illustrate the definition. The tags carry meta-information, that is, information about the information on the webpage. Common attributes are keywords, author and description. Note that these tags contain information about the information on the page, for example, what keyword categories the information belongs in.

A breakthrough in metadata would be a metaphysical advance in computing. XML is designed to do just that, but progress has been slow. XML is an HTML extension, Extensible Markup Language. Other advances are XMI, which is XML Metadata Interchange, and CWMI, the Common Warehouse Metamodel Interchange.

In the *Death of E*, Fingar & Aronica note the need to communicate metadata if e-business is to reach its potential: "Metadata interchange is essential to the continued growth of e-business, as data from increasingly diverse sources and applications needs to be exchanged both within the enterprise, and more importantly outside the enterprise across the value chain." So far, we exchange just text. We need a common semantics between companies, and we can't even do that within a company, so the breakthrough is not yet on the horizon.

8. Who am I?

Who am I? Sounds pretty straightforward, but it can be mind-numbingly complex. The complexity is not analytical in origin, psycho- or systems, but rather legal. Here's my situation. I am a person as you probably guessed, and I also have a small business that I started in 1996. In 1997, I incorporated my business, but I had a book contract and so I left the book with the small business and the rest of the business (consulting) shifted to the corporation. The corporation is called McDermott Computer Decisions, Inc, but I call it MCD, Inc for short. The corporate stockholders are myself and my girlfriend, and we are also corporate officers: I'm CEO, she's CFO, I'm Treasurer, she's General Secretary, I drive, she reads the map, she makes the pasta, I eat it, etc., etc.

Not that complicated yet, until the IRS gets involved. I, Patrick the person, file a 1040 that represents me the human being. My royalties and book expenses go on a schedule C or E, representing me the author. And the corporation files an 1120S. So every time I spend any money I have to go through the "Who am I?" routine. For example, when me the person is running a little short of cash, I can ask me the President of MCD, Inc. for an advance, which I invariably approve. Or I can suggest to me the President we declare a dividend and then vote as me the stockholder to ratify it. Either way, as CEO, I direct me the Treasurer to write a check to me the corporate employee, or me the stockholder, which I the person endorse and deposit into the bank account of me the person, withdraw some money and am on my way. I have to write or sign my name a dozen times to complete one of these transactions!

And of course, when I buy something, I have to figure out who (as in which me) bought it. Could it have been me the person? I hope not, since then it isn't tax deductible. What about a book? Am I using it as a reference for a book I'm writing or does the corporation want as a consultant's reference? Often, it's both. But if I bought it with my money, I have to get me to reimburse me. I haven't gone psycho yet, but I'm afraid one day I might disapprove one of my requests and start a big fight between me.

Of course the IRS also defines a person a bit differently from most people. For example, there is no such thing as an impersonal corporation because every corporation is a "Legal Person". And a married couple is one person, not two. That's why spouses are automatically responsible for each other's taxes—they are actually the same person as far as the IRS is concerned.

These distinctions may seem silly, but in fact they are important in data modeling and computer systems—not to mention in a tax audit. If your database is not designed to carry both spouses names in a tax system, or doesn't recognize that corporations are persons, your system might not be able to fulfill its requirements, or might be unnecessarily difficult to program. And you'll find Zen is probably the only way to understand the complexity. So watch for the sequel to this book.

Bibliography

I've listed here those books referred to in the text that you might find useful in your quest to learn about Zen and the Art of Systems Analysis.

Things Japanesey

Chamberlain, Basil Hall, *Japanese Things: Being Notes on Various Subjects Connected with Japan*, Rutland, Vermont: Charles E. Tuttle Company, 1971 (originally *Things Japanese*, 1905). ISBN: 0-8048-0713-2.

Dower, John W., *Embracing Defeat: Japan in the Wake of World War II*, New York: W.W. Norton, 1999. ISBN: 0-393-32027-8.

Lee, Bruce, *Chinese Gung Fu: The Philosophical Art of Self-Defense*, Santa Clarita, California: Ohara Publications, 1963. ISBN: 0-89750-112-8.

Musashi Miyamoto, Victor Harris, trans., *A Book of Five Rings*, Woodstock, New York: The Overlook Press, 1974 (1643). ISBN: 0-87951-018-8.

Okakura, Kakuzo, *The Book of Tea*, New York: Dover Publications, 1964 (1906). ISBN: 0-486-20070-1.

Yamamoto Tsunetomo, William Scott Wilson, trans., *Hagakure: The Book of the Samurai*, Tokyo: Kodansha International, 1979. ISBN: 4-7700-1106-7.

Things Programmatical

Beck, Kent, *Extreme Programming Explained: Embrace Change*, Reading, Massachusetts: Addison-Wesley, 2000. ISBN: 0-201-61641-6.

Beizer, Boris, *Software Testing Techniques, Second Edition*, New York: Van Nostrand Reinhold, 1990. ISBN: 0442245920.

Fowler, Martin, *Refactoring: Improving the Design of Existing Code*, Reading, Massachusetts: Addison-Wesley, 2000. ISBN: 0-201-48567-2.

Gamma, Erich, Richard Helm, Ralph Johnson & John Vlissides, *Design Patterns: Elements of Reusable Object-Oriented Software*, Reading, Massachusetts: Addison-Wesley, 1995. ISBN: 0-201-63361-2.

Hunt, Andrew & David Thomas, *The Pragmatic Programmer: From Journeyman to Master*, Reading, Massachusetts: Addison-Wesley, 2000. ISBN: 0-201-61622-X.

James, Geoffrey, *The Tao of Programming*, Santa Monica: Info Books, 1987. ISBN: 0-931137-07-1.

James, Geoffrey, *The Zen of Programming*, Santa Monica: Info Books, 1988. ISBN: 0-931137-09-8.

McDermott, Patrick, *Solving the Year 2000 Crisis*, Boston: Artech House, 1998. ISBN: 0-89006-725-2.

Riel, Arthur J., *Object-Oriented Design Heuristics*, Reading, Massachusetts: Addison-Wesley, 1996. ISBN: 0-201-63385-X.

McConnell, Steve, *Rapid Development: Taming Wild Software Schedules*, Redmond, Washington: Microsoft Press, 1996. ISBN: 1-55615-900-5.

Yourdon, Edward, *Rise & Resurrection of the American Programmer*, Upper Saddle River, New Jersey: Yourdon Press, 1996. ISBN: 0-13-121831-X.

Things Systems Developmental

Boehm, Barry, *Software Engineering Economics*, Upper Saddle River, New Jersey: Prentice Hall PTR, 1981. ISBN: 0-13-822122-7.

DeMarco, Tom & Timothy Lister, *Peopleware: Productive Projects and Teams*, New York: Dorset House Publishing Company, 1987. ISBN: 0-932633-05-6.

Hay, David C., *Data Model Patterns: Conventions of Thought*, New York: Dorset House, 1996. ISBN: 0932633293.

Larman, Craig, *Applying UML and Patterns: An Introduction to Object-Oriented Analysis and Design*, Upper Saddle River, New Jersey: Prentice Hall PTR, 1998. ISBN: 0-13-748880-7.

Moody, Fred, *I Sing the Body Electronic: A Year with Microsoft on the Multimedia Frontier*, New York: Penguin Books, 1995. ISBN: 0-14-017655-1.

Muller, Robert J. *Database Design for Smarties: Using UML for Data Modeling*, San Francisco: Morgan Kaufmann Publishers, 1999. ISBN: 1558605150.

Sharp, Alec & Patrick McDermott, *Workflow Modeling: Tools for Process Improvement and Application Development*, Boston: Artech House, 2001. ISBN: 1-58053-021-4.

Silverston, Len, William H. Inmon & Kent Graziano, *The Data Model Resource Book: A Library of Logical Data and Data Warehouse Designs*, New York: John Wiley & Sons, 1997. ISBN: 0471153648.

Yourdon, Edward, *Death March: The Complete Software Developer's Guide to Surviving "Mission Impossible" Projects*, Upper Saddle River, New Jersey: Prentice-Hall, 1997. ISBN: 0-13-748310-4.

Things Technological

Capra, Fritjof, *The Tao of Physics: An Exploration of the Parallels Between Modern Physics and Eastern Mysticism*, New York: Bantam Books, 1975. ISBN: 0-533-10868-9.

Cooper, Alan, *The Inmates Are Running The Asylum: Why High-Tech Products Drive Us Crazy and How to Restore the Sanity*, Indianapolis, Indiana: SAMS/Macmillan Computer Publishing, 1999. ISBN: 0-672-31649-8.

Ellul, Jacques, Geoffrey Bromiley trans., *The Technological Bluff*, Grand Rapids, Michigan: William B. Eerdsmans Publishing, 1990 (1986). ISBN: 0-8028-3678-X.

Koulopoulos, Thomas & Nathaniel Palmer, *The X-Economy: Profiting from Instant Commerce*, New York: Texere, 2001. ISBN: 1-58799-074-1.

Raskin, Jef, *The Humane Interface: New Directions for Designing Interactive Systems*, Reading, Massachusetts: Addison-Wesley Pub Co, 2000. ISBN: 0201379376.

Raymond, Eric S., *The Cathedral & The Bazaar: Musings on Linux and Open Source by an Accidental Revolutionary*, Sebastopol, California: O'Reilly, 1999. ISBN: 0-596-00108-8.

Shapiro, Carl & Hal Varian, *Information Rules: a Strategic Guide to the Network Economy*, Boston: Harvard Business Review Press, 1999. ISBN: 0-87584-863-X.

Turkle, Sherry, *Life on the Screen: Identity in the Age of the Internet*, New York: Touchstone, 1995. ISBN: 0-684-83348-4.

Things Eclectic

Booorstin, Daniel J., *The American Experience: The Democratic Experience*, New York: Vintage Books, 1973. 0-394-71011-8.

Johnson, Steven, *Emergence: The Connected Lives of Ants, Brains, Cities and Software*, New York: Scribner, 2001. ISBN: 0-684-86875-X.

Friedman, Thomas L., *The Lexus and the Olive Tree*, New York: Anchor Books, 2000. ISBN: 0-385-49934-5.

Hofstadter, Douglas R., *Le Ton beau de Marot: In Praise of the Music of Language*, New York: Basic Books, 1997. ISBN: 0-465-02475-0.

Krakauer, Jon, *Into Thin Air: A Personal Account of the Mount Everest Disaster*, New York: Anchor Books, 1997. ISBN: 0-385-49208-1.

Lamb, Brian, *Booknotes: America's Finest Authors on Reading, Writing, and the Power of Ideas*, New York: Times Books, 1997. ISBN: 0-8129-2847-4.

Lamott, Anne, *Bird by Bird: Some Instructions on Writing and Life*, New York: Anchor Books, 1994. 0-385-48001-6.

Lederer, William J. & Eugene Burdick, *The Ugly American*, New York: W.W. Norton, 1958. ISBN: 0-393-31867-2.

Minsky, Marvin, *The Society of Mind*, New York: Simon &Schuster, 1986. Smith, Adam, *An Inquiry into the Nature and Causes of The Wealth of Nations*, London: W. Strahan & T. Cadell in the Strand, 1776. (No ISBN).

Schary, Dore, *Mr. Blandings Builds His Dream House*, with Cary Grant, & Myrna Loy, Turner Broadcasting System, Inc., 1996 (1948). VHS.

Snow, C.P., *The Two Cultures*, Cambridge, United Kingdom: Cambridge University Press, 1998. ISBN: 0-521-45730-0.

Japanese Management

Deming, W. Edwards, *Out of the Crisis*, Cambridge, Massachusetts: The MIT Press, 2000 (1982). ISBN: 0-262-54115-7.

Imai, Masaaki, *Kaizen: The Key to Japan's Competitive Success*, New York: McGraw-Hill, 1986. ISBN: 0-07-554332-X.

Imai, Masaaki, *Gemba Kaizen: A Commonsense, Low-Cost Approach to Management*, New York: McGraw-Hill, 1997. ISBN: 0-07-031446-2.

Nonaka, Ikujiro & Hirotaka Takeuchi, *The Knowledge-Creating Company: How Japanese Companies Create the Dynamics of Innovation*, New York: Oxford University Press, 1995. ISBN: 0-19-509269-4.

Ouchi, William, *Theory Z: How American Business can meet the Japanese Challenge*, Reading, Massachusetts: Addison-Wesley, 1981. ISBN: 0-201-05524-4.

For A Good Story

Feynman, Richard P., *What Do You Care What Other People Think?: Further Adventures of a Curious Character*, New York: Bantam Books, 1988. ISBN: 0-553-34784-5.

Grove, Andy, *Only the Paranoid Survive: How to Exploit the Crisis Points that Challenge Every Company*, New York: Doubleday, 1999. ISBN: 0385483821.

Levy, Steven, *Insanely Great: The Life and Times of Macintosh, the Computer that Changed Everything*, New York: Penguin Books, 1994. ISBN: 0140291776.

Wilson, Mike, *The Difference between God and Larry Ellison—God doesn't Think He's Larry Ellison: Inside Oracle Corporation*, New York: William Morrow, 1997. ISBN: 0-688-14925-1.

About the Author

PATRICK McDERMOTT was a professional economist before he became a computer programmer, and so understands both Business Art and Systems Science, and connects the two in his writing and teaching. He is the author of *The Systems Analyst as Internal Consultant*, and co-author of *Workflow Modeling: Tools for Process Improvement and Application Development*, published by Artech House. His undergraduate degree was in Economics "with Honors" from The California State University at Sacramento, and he has a Master of Science in Information Systems from the University of San Francisco. He has a Professional Certificate in Computer Programming "with Distinction" from the University of California at Berkeley Extension and a Professional Award from The University of California at Santa Cruz Extension. He has been working in the Computer Industry for over twenty years, as a programmer, analyst, developer, consultant, manager and trainer. Employers have included the California Division of Labor Statistics & Research and American President Lines. He teaches seminars at the University of California, Berkeley and UCLA Extensions and programming classes at the College of Alameda. He is a member and former Director of the San Francisco Chapter of Data Management Association (DAMA). He runs his own consulting firm, MCD, Inc, in Oakland, California, specializing in training and consulting on computer technology. He would appreciate any feedback you might care to share: **pmcdermott@msn.com**.

Index

0-595-25679-1

Printed in the United States
95170LV00004BB/40/A

9 780595 256792